"Bravo! A master storyteller and educator, Jim Warford, has taken his life experience and story and shared it with us in *The Chemistry of Culture*! The circle of teach/learn being one in A'o is an epiphany and, blended with building trust and brain research, makes this book a one-of-a-kind for educators, students, and all human beings. Thank you for sharing your story, research, and lessons learned with us so that we might practice what you have learned with our students and educators!"—Kirk J. Miller, Ed.D., educator, father, grandfather, executive director, School Administrators of Montana

"This book is a must-read for any educator who wants to improve the culture of their school and/or school district. Warford provides helpful, practical, concrete suggestions and recommendations as well as real-life examples on how to improve the culture of schools. Improving student learning outcomes requires a positive, nurturing school culture. This book provides valuable insights and will be of great value to educators who want to create a nurturing, positive culture of learning."—Dr. Sheila J. Harrison, associate superintendent, Tracy, California

"Many of us can share how public education has had a positive effect on our lives. Fewer, however, have a testimony that public education saved their life. Jim shares his life story and then weaves examples of how we can make public education work for *all* kids. Ironically there is a Mrs. Jones in my 'circle.' Jim's candid personal history brought memories of what great educators meant in my life. Our profession is richer because of people like Jim Warford."—Benny Lile, Ed.D., superintendent, Metcalfe County Kentucky Schools

"Jim Warford knows why good teachers and administrators are the center of quality learning because he has lived that reality. Jim's knowledge and expertise certainly were embodied from his own passion for teaching and his own journey in the educational system."—Richard Hardy, AP Social Studies teacher, Brevard, North Carolina

"It is delightful to recommend this book to everyone, educators and business leaders alike. *The Chemistry of Culture* draws on scholars and scientists from numerous fields and Jim's extensive experiences in education and coaching. Jim came to Taiwan to lead our Environmental Education Empowerment Workshop. During the workshop, Jim promoted best practices in education and culture with environmental education experts from China and Japan. The workshop was remarkable and memorable, and I recommend this book based on my personal experience working with him."—Dr. Pin-Chih Wang, deputy secretary general, Taiwan Center for Corporate Sustainability, and lecturer at Chung Yuan University, Taiwan

"The Culture Framework outlined in this book is genius and long overdue! Jim Warford's insight into the world of education is based on years of experience whose impact for me started as his student in the classroom then later as a principal when he was superintendent of schools in Marion County, Florida. At all levels he has put culture before strategy, leading to innovative and proven results. This book is a must-read!"—Mark Vianello, CTE executive director, Marion County, Florida

"From Appalachia to the Aloha State, Jim Warford shares his personal journey in this book. Along the way, we are reminded that when a teacher truly believes in a student's ability to learn in the classroom, it can change his or her life forever and 'close that circle.' Drawing from his experiences both as a student and educator, Warford discusses the importance of creating a positive school culture that breeds teacher and student success by focusing on three essential elements (trust, empowerment, and collaboration) and provides the reader with strategies and examples. Jim Warford is a good storyteller, and this book is essential reading for any school administrator who has embraced school culture as a tool to help everyone at a school become better—including themselves."—Alan Ramos, principal, P. M. Wells Charter Academy

"When I first met Jim Warford, more than thirty-five years ago, I knew I had met someone really special. After working with him and having him teach my children, I am more convinced of this fact. Jim has a unique perspective and an uncanny knack for recognizing the real issues in education. He has the talent to connect with educators, evaluate situations, and zero in on solutions. *The Chemistry of Culture* is an evidence-based work that will surely have a profound impact on educators in every discipline. It belongs in the 'tool box' of every educator."—Diana Meierhenry, math teacher, Ocala, Florida

"Technology is driving social, economic, and cultural changes at an exponential rate and is already radically changing the time, place, and space for teaching and learning. In his work, *The Chemistry of Culture: Brain-Based Strategies to Create a Culture of Learning*, Jim Warford takes us into the real world of growing culture. By building relationships and changing our teaching mindset to become more relevant, we gain success and more rigorous learning for all of our students. Jim takes you on the journey of building real relationships with leaders, teachers, and students to demonstrate the impact of positive culture, trust, and powerful strategies that work across cultures in every setting. Jim has laid out the proof of the power of a culture of learning that will transfer anywhere."—Dr. Erik Swanson, superintendent, Omak, Washington

"Educator or not, *The Chemistry of Culture* is a *must*-read! Jim Warford was my 'Mary Kay Jones.' I also come from a poor, rural family with a mentally handicapped brother to care for. I was what we called a 'latchkey kid' because my mother and stepfather worked from sun up to sun down, so *all* household responsibilities, as well as making sure my brother was cared for and fed, were mine. I was an adult *long* before I should have been. School was my escape from reality, and Jim allowed me the glorious opportunity each day to be a creative, carefree child, while teaching me that learning could be *fun*. He loved and believed in me, even when I didn't feel I was worthy. Jim Warford's passion for education is truly unparalleled. His knowledge and excitement leap off the pages! Every person in my circle is receiving a copy!"—Lisa Dunham, Martinshöhe, Germany

"Jim Warford is one who truly understands 'technology-enhanced education' and the importance it plays in student engagement. But one does not get this engagement, unless 'environmental chemical reactions' are taking place! Jim hits it out of the park in this well-written, easy-to-read book on creating an environment of 'trust and joy'!"—Dr. James P. Bouché, district administrator, Lakeland Union High School District, Minocqua, Wisconsin

"Jim Warford is a masterful leadership coach. He recognizes that culture is key to effective schools and must be shaped for each unique school—not adopted by a rigid formula. He always seeks to understand before sharing his wisdom. In every great relationship, both parties gain. Farrington High School improved its school culture because of his shared wisdom, but clearly Jim Warford has learned lessons from the relationship as well as he shares his insights on shaping unique school cultures."—Dr. Richard Jones, senior consultant, Successful Practices Network

"Jim Warford is one of the most dedicated individuals that I have ever met in education. His passion for the work surrounding rigor, relevance, and relationships is uncontested. His work with our district helped push us closer to meeting our vision of *all* students being college and career ready. He is a captivating speaker and his ability to make the work applicable to all stakeholders is and continues to be a blessing to all those that come in contact with him."—Kenny Rodrequez, Ed.D., superintendent of schools, Grandview, Missouri

The Chemistry of Culture

The Chemistry of Culture

Brain-Based Strategies to Create a Culture of Learning

Jim Warford

ROWMAN & LITTLEFIELD
Lanham • Boulder • New York • London

Published by Rowman & Littlefield
An imprint of The Rowman & Littlefield Publishing Group, Inc.
4501 Forbes Boulevard, Suite 200, Lanham, Maryland 20706
www.rowman.com

6 Tinworth Street, London, SE11 5AL, United Kingdom

British Library Cataloguing in Publication Information Available

Library of Congress Cataloging-in-Publication Data

Names: Warford, Jim, 1947– author.
Title: The chemistry of culture : brain-based strategies to create a culture of learning / Jim Warford.
Description: Lanham : Rowman & Littlefield, [2019] | Includes bibliographical references. | Summary: "Neuroscientists are discovering the Chemistry of Culture by revealing the neurological links between our brain and our relationships. This book brings that brain research out of the lab and into schools by connecting it to highly effective culture-building strategies"—Provided by publisher.
Identifiers: LCCN 2019012313 (print) | LCCN 2019980987 (ebook) | ISBN 9781475851632 (cloth : alk. paper) | ISBN 9781475851649 (pbk. : alk. paper) | ISBN 9781475851724 (ebook)
Subjects: LCSH: Learning, Psychology of. | Interpersonal relations. | Reflective learning. | Human behavior. | Brain research.
Classification: LCC LB1060 W36 2019 (print) | LCC LB1060 (ebook) | DDC 370.15/23—dc23
LC record available at https://lccn.loc.gov/2019012313
LC ebook record available at https://lccn.loc.gov/2019980987

To my wonderful wife, Susan, you are the love and light of my life.
For more than forty years, you have walked with me, inspired me,
and trusted me. We have made some bold leaps together!
And I am always better because of you.

To my children, Nathan, Katie, and Lucas, you are a doctor, a teacher,
and a musical artist. Most importantly, you are all good, kind,
empathetic people. No father could be prouder. I learned as much
about what school should be from you as from anyone.
You gave me a lifelong goal: make every classroom and school
a place where I would want you to learn.
To my grandchildren, Javier and Nora Bonillia-Warford,
I hope this book will help more schools to create cultures of learning
to engage you and be filled with teachers who will
keep your love of learning alive.

To my father, the amazing Floyd Blair—well, technically you're my
father-in-law, but you're the only father I've ever known.
You've crammed ten normal lifetimes into your ninety-nine years.
Keep on learning!

Contents

Born in rural Kentucky poverty, Jim Warford's passion for teaching is driven by his compelling personal story. Jim's deep commitment to our schools led to a long and distinguished career as a courageous educational leader who pushes our thinking while keeping us focused on our students. He continues that tradition in this book by providing powerful examples around how to create a positive culture in schools, while recognizing the need to pivot that culture to embrace brain-based strategies in our instructional program.

I first met Jim fifteen years ago when he was named Florida's first chancellor of K–12 public schools. Since that time, I have watched him transform into a highly sought-after speaker and consultant for the International Center for Leadership in Education. He has worked with individual teachers, principals, superintendents, and everyone in between to help create instructional practices, programs, and policies that have enabled all students to receive a rigorous and relevant educational experience. But Jim chooses to spend the majority of his time in classrooms, with teachers, because he knows that's where it matters most.

Both Jim and I have learned through our work with schools across America and internationally that "Culture Trumps Strategy." Knowing that basic lesson, Jim has focused his work on helping schools to create a positive, innovative culture. Getting your culture right first is central to what we find that all of the nation's most rapidly improving schools have effectively done.

The Chemistry of Culture provides specifics on how Farrington High School in Hawaii has been so successful at creating such an innovative culture. That success has propelled Farrington to become a three-time national Model School. Located in one of Honolulu's poorest and most diverse neighborhoods, Farrington has created a culture of trust, empowerment, and collaboration through a teacher-led effort.

Jim provides specific strategies teachers and principals can use to improve the culture of their classroom or school. These strategies are based on discoveries coming from the field of neuroscience about how the chemistry of our brain is linked to our relationships and culture. These new discoveries highlight the importance of *trust* in school culture. Our desire and ability to trust each other has been hardwired into our DNA by evolution. Our ability to work together and teach each other has played a pivotal role in the survival of our species. The science says building trust can be learned and improved with practice.

In this book, Jim brings the brain research out of the lab and into schools. Readers will learn how to apply these strategies from principals and teachers who are using them. Readers will learn *why* culture is too important to be left to chance and how a positive school culture can be built by design. Readers will learn how to use these strategies to "bathe brains" in the neurochemicals needed to improve the culture of any school or classroom.

Dr. Bill Daggett, founder and chairman
International Center for Leadership in Education

Preface

All I ever really wanted to be was a teacher—a good teacher. You see, teachers didn't just change my life in some soft, education-speak sort of way. They saved it literally. They set it on the right course—this course. The course that brought me to you, dear reader. If I'm lucky enough that you are holding this book (or device) in your hands right now, I must thank a teacher, many teachers.

I was born a prisoner of poverty on the edge of Appalachian Kentucky. Teachers freed me. My mother found herself pregnant with me at thirteen. I never knew my father, never spoke to him. He stayed around us only long enough to father my sister, Billie Lynn, who was born fourteen months later. By age fifteen, my mother was an unmarried school dropout with two children.

In the vernacular of that rural Kentucky place and time, my mother was a "fallen woman." Those words don't have much meaning today, but my mother knew exactly what they meant. And she carried their pain to her early grave.

There were no community or government programs to help. Neither Oprah nor Dr. Phil were doing TV shows to help my mother cope with her situation. Didn't matter anyway. We couldn't have seen them. We didn't have a TV or indoor plumbing in the house where I was born. We were often passed to relatives and friends while my mother looked for work. Eventually, we came to live with our grandparents on their farm, while our mother went to work at the sprawling General Electric factories of Appliance Park outside Louisville, Kentucky, making appliances she could not afford.

When I was about nine, my mother married, and we moved to a house closer to town. I mostly remember my stepfather as angry, often violent, and given to fits of rage. You never knew what might set him off. For sure, my mother got the worst of it. Our home was a nightmare from which school was my constant escape . . . even though I was not a particularly good student.

You see, I dragged all the drama at home to school with me each day, often acting up or acting out. Do you have any students like that in your classroom today? Maybe that helps explain why I've so often been drawn to work with struggling students and schools. I saw the tragic power of poverty to shape children's lives up close and personal. I saw how the lack of education can give the children of poverty a lack of choices. I saw how the children of poor and uneducated parents can so early, and so easily, be condemned to continuing the cycle, closing the same sad circle. Their story would be my story . . . were it not for teachers.

Even though, on the outside, I was a difficult student, school was my escape, my refuge. It was a place of security, stability, and safety. Mostly, it was a place with clear rules. Even though I pushed back, and sometimes broke them, I now understand that I was actually glad the rules were there. As a teacher in my own classroom, that lesson served me well for many years and continues to serve me today. And I'll bet almost every teacher reading this can point to a moment like that, when a student comes back and tells you how much you meant to them. Many of you can quickly put a name and face to that memory. And so often, it's the students that surprise us. You often think to yourself, "Really? You're the one who comes back to thank me? I thought you hated school? Hell, I thought you hated me!" I've heard so many versions of that story through the years, but they all make us smile.

As a teenager, the abuse in our home escalated. More than anything, I wanted to save my mother and sister from the fear I saw in their eyes. My adolescent brain filled with sometimes violent thoughts of how I could do that. Had I acted on them, it would have sent my life in a completely different direction than the one that brought me to you. Do you understand what I'm saying?

But a teacher saved me. Specifically, it was the relationship she built with me that saved me. Her name was Mary Kay Jones, and she was my chorus teacher. She built such a caring relationship with me that, for the very first time, I felt safe to share the details of my home life, how I felt, and what I was thinking about doing to save my mother and sister.

At that moment, Mary Kay acted without hesitation. At the worst point in my life, she took me into her home and family and gave me a break from the drama of my home. She allowed me to see what a stable family looked like. Amazingly, to this day, she does not fully acknowledge the extraordinary gift she gave me. I became a better student because of her and our trusting relationship.

Mary Kay had her students performing almost constantly for school, community, and church events. She took us to concerts and plays in Louisville. She exposed me to a world I didn't know existed. More than anything, I wanted to meet her expectations, to please her, even more than my football coach! I believe she got me through high school and into college. How do you repay such a gift? To this day, I often feel like I'm still trying to close that circle.

Again, I know many of you understand exactly what I mean. So who's your Mary Kay Jones? What did she, or he, do for you? How did that teacher make such an impact on you? Have you reached out to let them know? If that teacher had such a big impact that you are a teacher today, are you a Mrs. Jones to a child? How do you know? What makes you think so? Have you shared your story with others, closed your circle?

That's what I want to do in this book: close my own circle. You see, throughout my life I've had the enormous privilege of learning from great teachers and principals. For the past twenty years, I've had the opportunity to join schools on their journey from struggling to successful, sometimes as the teacher, other times as the student, always as a learner. I've cheered as some of these schools made a bold decision: to become a Model School! I've shared their struggles and celebrated their successes. Mostly, I've learned.

Acknowledgments

I am deeply indebted to the many teachers, principals, and coaches who have had such an impact on my life and my learning. I wrote this book in part to say thank you and to close my own circle of A'o. Sadly, there are not enough pages to bring all of you into the book. But you know who you are!

Mahalo nui loa (thank you very much) to the staff and students of Farrington High School in Honolulu for allowing me to share their inspiring journey these past four years. It has been the most rewarding professional experience of my life. And I can truthfully say that I've learned far more from Farrington than Farrington has learned from me. For that reason, all royalties from the sale of this book will go to a special student fund at Farrington High School.

My deepest gratitude to Dr. Bill Daggett, Dr. Linda Lucey, Kris Ross, Ray McNulty, Dr. Richard Jones, and my many colleagues at the International Center for Leadership in Education (ICLE). The Rigor/Relevance Framework is my map to locate good teaching and learning. It has helped me find "True North" in the classroom for twenty-five years.

Thank you to the talented staff at Rowman & Littlefield who believed in this project and helped bring it to life: Dr. Tom Koerner, Sarah Jubar, and Emily Tuttle. Thank you for your expertise, patience, and timely support.

Finally, I want to thank Rachel Fugo for her patient technical assistance helping me prepare this manuscript for the publishers. Not so sure I could have met my deadlines without her.

Introduction

Closing the Circle of A'o

I want to start by saying a special thank you, or Mahalo, to Hawaiian language teacher Illiahi Doo (ill-e-ah-he). It was Mr. Doo who first taught me that, in the Hawaiian language, there is only one word for both teaching and learning: A'o (pronounced ah-oh). Mr. Doo went on to explain that, in the ancient Hawaiian culture, not only is there only one word for both teaching and learning, but they were also not seen as separate things. They were seen as the same thing, as different sides of the same coin, as different links in the same circle.

More importantly, Mr. Doo is teaching me that in the Hawaiian culture, whenever one learns new knowledge, one also receives a responsibility to pass that knowledge on, to teach it to others. This ancient concept of the "oneness" of teaching and learning immediately resonated with me, and the more I learned, the more I wanted to understand. I find there's something inherently beautiful about the Hawaiian culture—their language, their spirit of Aloha. There is a duality of purpose that shows up in A'o and other elements of their communication that is powerful. It articulates a connectivity to teaching/learning (A'o) and greeting/farewell and love/affection (Aloha).

I want to be clear about this. One of the main reasons I wrote this book is because I believe there are lessons—important lessons—that those of us on the mainland can learn from Hawaii. I believe these lessons go way beyond the classroom and schoolhouse. They can help us reconnect with one another. And I believe we need these lessons more now than at any point in my seventy-year life!

Maybe I'm reaching here, but I think this ancient Hawaiian duality captures a circular connectivity that is too often lost between teacher and learner. It captures what it means to greet the arrival of children each day with the success of their departure in mind. To approach them always, despite the challenges they bring to our door, with love and compassion. And I hope for you to see that this A'o connection extends in every direction between us all—principal, teacher, and student. Do we greet our teachers each day that same way, with the success of their departure in mind? Maybe you think I'm just rambling . . . but just maybe . . . you get it. I hope so. Because that's exactly what I want to explore in this book.

Let me give you a concrete example. I've worked with hundreds of struggling schools. One of the first essential questions I ask everyone is: *Do you believe all children can learn?* Certainly, they can't all learn in the same way, on the same day, and at the same rate. But do you believe they *all* can learn? The research is crystal clear. Until the answer to this question is yes, we are stuck.

My next question in these schools is: *Do you believe all teachers can learn?* Surprisingly, I don't hear yes nearly as often. Why is that? How can so many school leaders speak so passionately about all children learning, yet have so little faith in the adults in the building? These two simple questions reveal a great deal about a school's culture. You see, it's not enough to believe our students can learn. We must also believe our teachers can learn.

Imagine, if you will, a school where every person comes each day to learn—students and teachers alike. A school where students are learning from teachers but also from other students, where teachers are learning from other teachers . . . and also from students! This is what I mean by a learning school. This book is about how we can create a culture where *all* can learn, a school of teaching and learning, a school of A'o. A school where everyone has a Growth Mindset, where everyone is learning. In this book you will discover just such a school, and you will learn how it came to be that way.

This book will also connect culture to the most recent discoveries about the chemistry of our brain and how brain chemistry connects to the daily actions, and interactions, in our classrooms and schools. These new discoveries dramatically highlight the importance of trust in our school culture. They show that our desire and ability to trust each other has been hardwired into our DNA by millions of years of evolution; that our ability to work together, and teach each other, has played the most important role in the survival of our species; and why learning to build trust with each other is, ultimately, in the best interest of all of us.

This book will bring that research out of the lab and into your school or classroom. You will learn how to apply these strategies from school leaders

and teachers who are already using them. They will share what has worked and, more importantly, what has not. I'm deeply in debt to these educators for sharing their journey with us. From them, you will learn why culture is too important to be left to chance and that a positive school culture must be intentionally built. You will learn how you can use these strategies to literally "bathe brains" in the neurochemicals needed to improve the culture of any school.

You will find in part II of this book a collection of research- and brain-based strategies for creating this culture of learning. These strategies, and the leadership characteristics associated with them, are taken directly from emerging discoveries in the field of neuroscience. They can be used by anyone to improve the culture in their classroom, school, or district.

Another link in our circle of A'o will connect these most advanced discoveries in neuroscience to the wisdom of an ancient Hawaiian culture that stretches back well over a millennium. It was a voyaging culture, whose concept of A'o produced knowledge so strong, it brought them thousands of miles across the world's greatest ocean to settle a small string of volcanic islands on the most isolated archipelago in the world . . . long before Europeans would dare such a feat.

This is also a book about Farrington High School, in inner-city Honolulu, one of Hawaii's most diverse and poorest schools. We will follow Farrington's journey from struggling inner-city high school to twice being named a National Model School, a school where visitors from across Hawaii and the mainland instantly recognize that there is something special about the culture being built there, a unique culture of teaching and learning, of A'o.

But Farrington will not be alone. The impact of their highly effective, teacher-led culture of A'o has inspired their feeder schools to begin their own journey. In this book, you will get to see the impact of a fully articulated vision of trust, collaboration, and empowerment across K–12. Some of the strategies in part II of this book will demonstrate how this highly effective culture is allowing teachers to innovate, create, and actually reinvent classrooms in the Kalihi community from kindergarten to twelfth grade.

Full disclosure here: I've worked with literally hundreds of schools and teacher groups over the years. And to paraphrase John Steinbeck in *Travels with Charley*, for many schools I have great admiration, some even affection, but for Farrington it is love. And it's hard to analyze love when you're in it. Farrington became a National Model School by building a culture of teaching and learning, a culture of A'o. Like the audiences who've seen their sessions at Model Schools or visited their campus, they have inspired and energized me.

I can honestly say I've learned more from them than they've learned from me. In this book, you will learn how Farrington is the link in our circle that connects all the rest, from the ancient wisdom of A'o to the more effective leadership strategies emerging from the field of neuroscience. Most importantly, from Farrington we will learn how their positive culture helped turn both current brain research and ancient wisdom into everyday practice.

Farrington has put into practice an idea I first heard from my friend Dr. Dick Jones that school leadership is not a *position*, but rather a *disposition* for taking action, or, as they say at Farrington, making shift happen! Farrington is learning that in a culture with the right Growth Mindset, every teacher can be a leader, and Farrington has turned more teachers into leaders than any school I've seen. How did they start? By getting their priorities in order. The guiding vision at Farrington High School is Relationships, Relevance, and Rigor. Why that order?

Because if your culture is broken you can't fix anything else, and even if your culture is not broken, it is only as strong as your foundation, and every foundation must be built on strong, positive relationships. For twenty years, I've watched schools learn this the hard way. I've studied and watched schools attempt to implement changes of all kinds only to fail because they ignored this simple truth or thought they could skip right over it. The question of why culture is so important is so essential that we will devote the entire next chapter to exploring it. Farrington High School did not ignore it. They thought deeply about it. They planned strategically for it. They budgeted for it. They invested time in it. And they improved it in measurable ways.

From Farrington we will also learn the necessity of linking our efforts to create a positive school culture for teachers directly to creating a positive culture of learning for all students in our classrooms. And that is one of our first lessons from Farrington. All means all. The circle of A'o must include students, teachers, administrators, and community. Farrington learned a true culture of learning can't be built overnight. It can't be mandated from the top. It must be grown from the ground up, organically, one classroom at a time. Yes, that takes time. But more importantly, it takes focus and strategic thinking.

This book also owes a great big Hawaiian Mahalo to Farrington principal Al Carganilla, strategic planner Cindy Werkmeister, teacher leadership cadre coordinator Jessica Kato, and many others. You will hear from each of them in this book as they share their Model School journey with you. They will share specific culture-building strategies, processes, and protocols Farrington has developed. Hopefully, you will come to understand how they have made Hawaii's Aloha spirit truly alive and real, and I hope this book will tell that story.

The Power of Mental Models

But as passionate as I am about the Farrington story, I must confess to feeling somewhat reluctant to write this book or any book, in part because a book needs readers, and everywhere I go in my work today, I find teachers feeling more overwhelmed and more frustrated than ever before. And almost everyone, everywhere, speaks of having no time. Our world moves faster and faster while we feel further behind. As a result, many people just don't read as much anymore or they read shorter things. A book takes a big chunk of time! So, if you're still with me here on this page, Mahalo, or thank you! Your time is precious, and I will try not to waste it.

But I've learned that, as a group, teachers do read more than others, and we often get attached to our favorite books. I enjoy all kinds of books, but my favorites are the ones that change me forever, in some deep and fundamental way. They change me by changing the way I see the world. Books like Robert Pirsig's *Zen and the Art of Motorcycle Maintenance*. It may not be the best example because, well . . . it's not exactly an easy read, but it's a book that once read, you can't un-read.

Books like *Zen* give us a new perspective from which to see the same things we've seen before. It gave me a new "mental model," which gave me a new way to see how things work, and in that new way of seeing lies the learning. By seeing a thing from new perspectives, we gain a deeper understanding of that thing than we had before.

Let's do a simple thought experiment. We've all seen a memorable sunrise or sunset. Think of one. Try to remember how it looked. Hold that thought. Now for thousands of years we believed the world was flat, the center of the universe, and the sun revolved around the earth. Now, back to your memory. Ask yourself this question: if the earth was flat and the sun *was* actually revolving around us, how would it look different? Think about that a minute. I'll model wait time.

If this was a classroom, I would not answer. We'd explore your thinking and then do some metacognition by thinking about your thinking. But this is a book and I can't hear you. So the answer is: it would look exactly the same! But our answer depends on our mental model. Our mental model determines whether we will see the sun revolving around the earth or the earth revolving around the sun.

Sadly, for most of human history, mental models were all we had to answer those big questions and changing mental models can be difficult and dangerous work. Mental models are very, very powerful. If you think about it, throughout history a struggle over mental models is the root cause of what we've most often fought wars about. We sometimes forget the terrible price many scientists paid—and continue to pay—to make sure our mental models are built on facts, evidence, and reason.

To be honest, that's another goal I have for this book: I hope to give you a new mental model that will change the way you see your school's culture and, from that new perspective, give you a better understanding of (1) the fact that if your culture is broken, you can't fix anything else and (2) how to build a new culture based on teaching and learning, a culture of A'o.

If you find something useful in these pages, it will come from the A'o I've shared with teachers and principals along the way. Together, we've learned that if you want to create change of any lasting kind in a school, it helps to begin by changing the way you see your culture. Adopting a new mental model or map to guide your change is an important first step. As we just saw, by changing your mental model of anything, you can learn to see that thing in a new way. Our mental models are some of the most powerful forces in our lives. We will explore much more about that in chapter 5.

To change your culture, the first thing you will need is a new mental model of what your culture should look like, and we will explore one new model in this book. This new model of culture is based on the idea that a culture of teaching and learning, a culture of A'o, a culture built on a foundation of positive relationships, is built with three things: trust, empowerment, and collaboration. This is a book about how to improve those three things.

It was my high school teacher Mary Kay Jones who first taught me about the importance of relationships in the classroom. In my work with ICLE, I learned to focus on rigor and relevance. But from Mary Kay Jones, I learned that the proper order is relationships then relevance because only when the first two are in place can we hope to reach rigor for all students.

I also learned a lot about the power of relationships and building a positive culture from my principal, Ken Vianello, at Vanguard High School in

Ocala, Florida. Mr. Vianello was a big, outgoing Italian from Chicago whose warmth and enthusiasm were infectious. Mr. V's smile was as big as our school gym, and it totally transformed our school—and my life. Ken was my first leadership mentor. Later, as superintendent, I became his boss. But until his death, he remained and will always be Mr. Vianello to me.

I want to add Mr. Vianello to our circle of teaching and learning by sharing something special he did that I will never forget. Mr. V was my principal for fifteen years, and of all the recognition and awards I've received in my career, I am most proud of the fact that during those years my fellow teachers at Vanguard High School chose me as their Teacher of the Year three separate times. The final time, in 1997, I was also selected as our district's Teacher of the Year.

Because I had learned to trust Mr. V, I began to share my personal story with him, my troubled childhood, and what Mary Kay Jones had done for me. He understood that my story was what made me the teacher I was becoming. He also knew that, because it was so painful, I'd not spoken about it with others. He urged me to share it publicly for the first time. He believed other teachers needed to hear it. He knew it would be hard, and I knew he was right. What I didn't know was that prior to the ceremony Mr. Vianello contacted Mary Kay Jones in Kentucky, and he secretly made arrangements to bring her to our school in Ocala, Florida.

I was teaching in my classroom one day just before the Teacher of the Year Awards when Mr. V's voice came on the intercom calling me to the office. When I got there, he asked me if I was prepared for the District's Awards Ceremony that coming Friday. The Golden Apple Awards are still a big event in Ocala. There were fifty schools in the Marion County School District. The awards are done with lots of flash in a big auditorium and, yes, I was nervous. Mostly about what I would say . . . if I should get the chance. I'd never before spoken about my mother, my home life, or Mary Kay Jones in public and was not sure I could get through it and remain composed.

Mr. Vianello suggested I get back to class and that he would walk with me. When we got back to my room, he opened the door . . . and there stood Mary Kay Jones in the middle of the room, surrounded by my students! In that moment, I knew Mr. Vianello had closed an important circle, a circle that was very real for me. Ultimately, I hope this book is a tribute to Mary Kay Jones, Mr. Vianello, and all the teachers and principals who've taught me, the teachers with whom I've taught, and the teachers I am now teaching and coaching. I am grateful to have learned from each of you. This is a book about A'o: teaching and learning.

Part One

Why Culture Matters

The most important question a student will ever ask a teacher is: why do I need to know this? The most important question a teacher can ask a principal is: why do I need to do this? If we don't have good answers for those question, we're in trouble before we start. Why does culture matter? Because if your culture is broken, you can't fix anything else. At the same time, more educators are also beginning to understand the corollary to this axiom, which is if your culture is broken, you can't *implement* anything else.

And yet failed or poorly executed implementations are literally everywhere. A failed implementation simply means that after two or three years of effort, the program, technology, or model either has not taken root or not survived at all. For example, it is not uncommon to visit a school with a large English Language Learner population where you are told all teachers have been trained in GLAD Instructional Strategies, only to find little evidence of them being used in classrooms.

Those who are charged with monitoring the return on the investment in new programs, curricula, technology, or school improvement models are often the first to learn why culture matters. One of the easiest ways to get agreement from any group of school leaders around a table is to say: "It's all about the implementation." Without exception, people will nod their heads in agreement. It's become a cliché you've heard over and over. Meanwhile, schools and districts continue to lurch from one poorly implemented program to the next.

The reality is that a number of studies have shown an extremely high failure rate for the implementation of the majority of new programs or initiatives across the country. A 2018 study by the U.S. Education Department reported on the effectiveness of $1.5 billion spent on a variety of programs in reading, writing, math, and science instruction. Results showed that only twelve of the sixty-seven promising new programs, or 18 percent, were found to have any positive impact on student achievement. A prior 2013 study also found that when education reforms were put to rigorous scientific tests with control groups and random assignment, 90 percent of them failed to find positive effects. We must ask ourselves why.

A Lesson from Technology

Technology in the classroom has been one of the shiniest new toys to grab our attention. Across the country, school leaders have spent billions of dollars and countless hours on a dizzying array of technology devices and programs, sometimes followed by well-publicized disasters such as the Los Angeles Unified School District's billion-dollar iPad initiative. Yet, during classroom visits in school after school, you will still see traditional stand-and-deliver instruction the majority of the time. Why is that?

Clearly there were innovative teachers using technology, even "flipping" their classes years ago. There were true pioneers like Paul Andersen at Bozeman High School in Bozeman, Montana, using technology to totally reinvent their classrooms. But honestly, most of these early innovators had no idea what they were doing. There were no maps, guides, or Mental Models to show them the way. Most were just fortunate enough to have an innovative principal like Ken Vianello who trusted them enough to let them try. At first, they failed more often than they succeeded.

But today, not only do we have far better tools and devices, we have the strategies we need to help us use them well. We absolutely know *how* to do it. Wes Kieschnick, a senior fellow at the International Center for Leadership in Education, has written what is perhaps the definitive book about how to use technology in the classroom. *Bold School* is a brilliant, step-by-step guide that combines the best of old school teaching with innovative blended learning technology integration. In *Bold School*, Mr. Kieschnick provides us with multiple strategies to demonstrate how any teacher, at any grade level, in any content area, can use technology to make their instruction more rigorous, relevant, and engaging.

The point is, if we know what to do and we know how to do it, why don't we do it more often? Why don't we make our schools more engaging for all our students? We have been talking about the need for twenty-first-century instruction for, let's see . . . nineteen years now. We'll soon be a quarter of the way into the twenty-first century. When will the majority of our class-rooms and schools begin to look like it?

Think for a minute of your own school. How many of your classrooms look like they're ready for this century? More importantly, are they exciting places where students want to be? Are they classrooms where you're genuinely excited to send your children? Your *own* children? If your answer to that question is any version of "not so much," ask yourself why, and please keep reading.

This Too Shall Pass

If your culture is broken, you can't fix anything else!

It's easy to understand that some of you may still be somewhat skeptical about all this "culture" stuff. After all, in this era of Data Teams, it can sound pretty soft and squishy. The truth is many school leaders only endured the talk about mission statements or values, quietly going through the motions to create compliance but secretly believing that, mostly, any time or money spent on that stuff was a waste. Hey, we're all adults here! We're profession-als! We know what we're supposed to do. Let's just get on with it! It was years ago that we first heard Bill Daggett say, "Culture eats strategy for lunch." But some of us didn't really buy it. Since then, and after many unsuccessful implementations, we've learned the hard way that Bill Daggett was right: Culture not only eats strategy for lunch but also breakfast and dinner!

The International Center for Leadership in Education (ICLE) has spent more than twenty-five years studying hundreds of schools and classrooms across this country, Europe, and Asia. The problem not only continues; it seems to have gotten worse—everywhere. Teachers and principals are more overwhelmed and frustrated than ever before. They face students whose brains are wired differently by technology. They must meet the demands of increasing numbers of helicopter parents. And they face ever higher piles of paperwork. Teaching has never been an easy job, but the pressures piled on today's teachers are unprecedented.

Racing to find a silver bullet, schools and districts simply increase the rate of change. No wonder teachers so often say, "This, too, shall pass"; they know they won't even finish the current implementation before beginning the next one. Next time you hear someone say that, look them right in the eye and say, "You're right!" Of course it will. It almost always has. Why? Because if your culture is broken, you can't fix anything else. And too many school cultures are, if not broken, damaged or dysfunctional.

The pervasive power of a "this too shall pass" school culture to resist any change often explains why so many school improvement plans ultimately have little impact on school performance. Culture is deeply embedded in the routines of any school. Any written plan, in and of itself, does little to change the mindsets and routines created by the existing culture. The existing culture can create a comfortable inertia that encourages staff to maintain their current and familiar practices rather than embrace new and unfamiliar ideas. Changing existing culture is most certainly a daunting task. But it is not a hopeless endeavor, as so many Model Schools have demonstrated.

This problem is certainly not confined to schools. Your school culture is rooted in the context of your community culture, and your community culture is rooted in the broader culture of our country. You don't need anyone to tell you that our country's culture has changed and that not all of the changes are for the better. We have access to more information, but not all of it is real. We communicate faster and more easily but not always more clearly. We watch the rate of change get faster and faster but often feel less sure it's in the right direction.

ICLE's work with hundreds of schools and districts across the country has given them the opportunity to study the process of implementation of a variety of initiatives in inner-city schools in Miami, New York, Los Angeles, Detroit, Chicago, and Atlanta and in many small towns and rural areas too. It's pretty close to a cliché to say, "It's all about the implementation" because so many school leaders readily agree. Then we must ask: why do implementations so often fail or have little lasting impact?

After some serious self-reflection, many schools are reaching the conclusion that their culture is, if not broken, at least not effective. Too many schools are beginning to understand that their culture is their biggest barrier to implementing any real change or school improvement. That's exactly how Bill Daggett began to understand the reality of what he had been saying about culture for years.

～

Culture eats strategy for lunch!

～

The answer to why the implementation of so many excellent initiatives fails or has so little lasting impact is simple. Schools need to fix their culture before they can fix anything else. The more you think about this and the closer you look, the clearer the problem will become. Too many schools often jump from one initiative or program to the next without ever attending to their root problem: culture.

Let's start by being more precise about what we mean by culture, what culture is, and what it is not. Your school's culture is *not* your stated mission and values. In fact, ICLE has learned that going through the process of writing down your vision, mission, and values will do almost nothing to improve your culture. Think about it. Almost every single school you can visit has done that. They've not only written them down but proudly point to where they're posted. But . . . it's a rare school where you can find a single person who can tell you what they are! How meaningful is that?

Your school's culture is driven by the collective attitudes, values, and beliefs of every individual in the building. These often "hidden" perspectives will determine the more visible behaviors that eventually become the observable aspects of school culture. The observable behaviors and relationships, when combined with the hidden values and beliefs, create the culture. A school's culture determines its collective personality.

But . . . whether you recognize it or not, your school has its own culture. When your school's culture is ignored, it might (if you're really, really lucky) evolve in a way that's good. But on the other hand, it might just as easily devolve into a culture that can drive away your best teachers, a culture that blocks all efforts at improvement. It can become a truly toxic environment that kills the spirit of all who enter. Yes, building a positive culture is hard, but the costs of not doing so can take a terrible toll.

It's a little like that gym membership, exercise bike, or NordicTrack (remember them?) that you bought to put in your basement or rec room. You know you need it! At first you were filled with good intentions. But then life happened. You had a hard time getting around to using it. It began to gather dust. Some of you started to hang clothes on it. But if you want to see the benefit, you have to work at it. It's the same with culture.

But it's not just schools. According to research done by the Boston consulting group PwC and reported in "Forging a Winning Corporate Culture," 75 percent of business transformations flat-out fail because of their corporate culture. In another recent study, "The Value of Corporate Culture," Luigi Guiso, Paola Sapienza, and Luigi Zingales of the Institute for Economics found that the existence of a defined set of corporate values made no difference to short- or long-term performance. The study found that spending time and money creating a well-wordsmithed vision and mission statement has little to no impact . . . unless you then become intentional and deliberate about turning those values into a positive and innovative culture.

The business world is leading and funding the research into culture because they have learned that a strong company culture has enormous benefits. In their new book, *Cultural Transformations: Lessons of Leadership and Corporate Reinvention*, John Mattone and Nick Vaidya cite companies like Zappos, Google, Apple, Wegmans, Graybar, Genpact, and Virtusa as having a strong and easily identifiable corporate culture. Research is showing that valued employees are more likely to refer other talented professionals they know when positions open up. The book lists six critical steps used in the business world to transform culture:

The Six Critical Steps from the Business World to Transform Culture

- *Culture starts with the CEO. Are you a CEO who "Thinks Different" and "Thinks Big"?*
- *Do you counter-balance "Thinking Different" and "Thinking Big" with heavy doses of humility? In other words, do you have the guts to be vulnerable and recognize that while you may be great in certain areas both individually and collectively as a company, you still have . . . gaps that need to be addressed to achieve greatness? Are you able to see and feel the pain associated with staying the same and are you able to get your team to see and feel the pain? People only consider changing when the pain associated with staying the same is perceived to be worse than the pain associated with change.*
- *Creating a compelling future for your people and teams? It starts with great leadership at all levels.*
- *Are you able to change mindsets? If you can change mindsets, you can change behavior. If you can change behavior, you will change results.*

- *Are you able to push the talent levers in support of your new culture?*
- *Are you passionate and diligent in measuring progress and course-correcting?*

So how do you get started? To begin, you must start with *why*. After more than twenty-five years of bringing Model Schools together to study and share, one of the most important lessons ICLE has learned about what makes them different is that Model Schools go slow at first so they can go faster later on. Have you heard that somewhere before?

One of the ways they go slow is by building a broader consensus about *why* they need to change before they jump to the what or how. They take more time to clearly define *why* it's in the best interest of all staff to embrace cultural change. It's important that everyone be able to understand the benefits of cultural change before they begin the process of changing it.

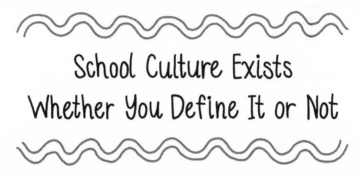

School Culture Exists Whether You Define It or Not

So exactly what is culture? The word "culture" is from the Latin word "cultis," which means care. Your school's culture is the accumulation of what your school cares about, the shared values, beliefs, and behaviors that define your school's daily interactions. In other words, your school culture is the unique collection of values that defines who you are and what is expected, accepted, and celebrated by your school. If building a positive culture sounds difficult, that's because it is.

Here's some good news: in this era of shrinking budgets, culture is free, or at least relatively inexpensive in terms of money. But it most certainly takes time and attention, both of which can be hard to come by without some cost. It helps when you begin to deeply understand that your culture is actually your most important asset. Taking the time to strategically and intentionally build a positive culture and making the effort to consistently model and measure the behaviors you "care" about will prove to be some of the most important things you can do.

So that leads us to the question of why some schools are so resistant to change, even when there is clear and compelling evidence that their culture is dysfunctional or even toxic. Whatever the current condition of your school, introducing cultural change is a long, challenging process. Most successful transformations ICLE has studied take three years minimum. One big barrier is that your school's current culture is a known quality. Your staff has an existing "mental model" and changing mental models is difficult (more about that in chapter 5). Even if people don't like it, they're familiar with it. For some people, any change can be threatening.

ICLE has been hosting Model Schools Conferences for more than twenty-five years and coaching schools on their way to becoming Model Schools. Often, these schools seem to implement so smoothly, to move so rapidly, so effectively. Over and over ICLE has found itself asking why. So, several years ago, ICLE began to study that question. Why are these schools able to implement change so effectively, while so many other schools struggle?

If you're still reading this book right now, you've probably asked yourself some version of that same question already. The answer is they fixed their culture first. Because . . . if your culture is broken, you can't fix anything else! And, if you've read this far, you've probably already asked yourself how. What exactly did they do?

If you attempt to implement reforms but fail to engage the culture of a school, nothing will change.

—Seymour Sarason, school reform researcher

For the rest of this book, we will explore this essential question: what do these Model Schools do differently? And we will explore some successful answers. We will share our A'o (teaching and learning) about culture from some of the schools who have given the International Center the enormous privilege of joining them on their journey from struggling to successful. With every school, and from each journey, ICLE has both taught and learned. To each of these schools, we are grateful. We will close this circle, and we will pass it on.

As we begin, it is important to remember there is not only wisdom in the concept of A'o, but practicality as well. We speak all the time, in many ways, about maintaining instructional focus, about being student-centered. But what does that really mean? How can we define it? Just maybe, the ancient Hawaiian concept of A'o offers a way to see our schools as a place where learning is shared between the teacher and the learner.

Imagine, if you will, a school where both the students and the adults come every day as learners—that is, they come to school with a learner's mind. The student comes to learn the knowledge of subject content; the teachers come to learn more about their content too but also more about the art and science of teaching. In such a school, maybe some of the teachers are open and able to learn not only with but from their students. And in this "learning school," it is a Growth Mindset that guides them all.

In a traditional school, students often learn passively from teachers. In a school filled with A'o, everyone is learning. Students learn from teachers but also from other students. More importantly, teachers learn from teachers but also from students. A school filled with A'o is a school filled with learners, a culture of learning. And this is often what best describes how a Model School is different. They've created a true culture of learning.

That is exactly what makes Farrington High School in Honolulu a Model School. When Farrington High School was shared with European colleagues in 2016 at the Making Shift Happen Conference in Amsterdam, it was the European school leaders that dubbed Farrington a "Learning School." And that's exactly what they are building at Farrington: a culture of learning for all. It's a culture where students often learn from other students, and teachers regularly learn from other teachers. At Farrington, teachers are empowered to plan and lead their own professional development. They are building a culture where A'o is practiced by all.

In this book, you will learn about Farrington's incredible journey. You will learn from them how they are transforming the culture of their school and influencing other schools. You will learn how they have created a truly student-centered culture. You will learn how their positive culture is based on building better relationships.

We began by asking why culture matters. Culture matters because it trumps strategy, budgets, and leadership. Because in a school culture where teachers, administrators, parents, and support staff all share a Growth Mindset and establish high expectations, students will rise to meet them. Unfortunately, the opposite is also true. If a school's culture doesn't establish a Growth Mindset and high expectations, fewer students will meet them.

From the neuroscience in chapter 3, we will learn more precisely how specific behaviors in highly effective school cultures stimulate certain chemicals and neurotransmitters in the brain and how these chemicals measurably increase the success and satisfaction felt by all involved. We will explore the growing body of neuroscientific research that demonstrates the impact of culture on our brains and the impact of our brains on our culture. The exciting part is that this new research is showing exactly how these brain chemicals help us build trust, form friendships, and work well together on a team.

The challenge for school leaders and teachers is to figure out what we can learn from neuroscience that we can use to build a better school and classroom culture, a culture where we're regularly releasing the right brain chemicals and reducing those that significantly inhibit learning. By better understanding just how chemicals like oxytocin activate the brain, you can intentionally design more opportunities to help you build a culture of trust for everyone—administrators, teachers, students, parents, and community.

Why does culture matter? Because a school's culture is the sum total of all the relationships within a school. Because if your culture is broken, you can't fix anything else. Because a school's culture matters most for its students. A school's culture establishes the norms of behavior and expectations. For our students, a school's culture becomes what they know of school and often the world. In short, the culture of your school will make or break your students' educational experience. That's why. So let's decide to make it a good one!

The Farrington Way:
A Culture of A'o

It's not possible to tell this story of A'o without also telling the story of Farrington High School in Honolulu. Not only because it is from Farrington that I learned about the ancient concept of A'o, but because it may be the "Farrington Way" that best brings the story to life. And there's no better way to start that story than with Farrington principal Al Carganilla. In a very real way, his story is their story because he has lived the Farrington Way.

Principal Alfredo Carganilla Jr., known as Al or Coach Al to most, was born to two immigrant parents from the Philippines. Al's older brother was born in the Philippines, but he and Al grew up with their parents in Honolulu's lower Kalihi neighborhood, not a mile from Farrington, where Al went to school. Both boys were latchkey kids growing up, as both their parents had two jobs each, often working fourteen to sixteen hours a day.

Despite often not being home for dinner with the boys, Al's parents almost never missed a baseball or basketball game. They left the responsibilities of school to the teachers and faculty, as many Filipino parents did, but were always very supportive of their sons by watching as many of their games as possible. Playing sports was a way for Al to feel safe and keep busy. After playing for Farrington High School, Al played baseball at the University of Hawaii under legendary coach Les Murakami.

What's clear to those who know Al best is that his parents planted the values of respect, hard work, responsibility, and humility deeply in his character. These are the values that not only shaped the person Al has become, but they are the values that he instills in Farrington today. Al embodies these values for the students and staff of Farrington High School and for all the young players that come through his Kalihi-based Go Nuts Baseball Club. Baseball is popular in Kalihi, and the Kalihi Go Nuts are recognized as a powerhouse throughout Hawaii. Al's twelve-year-old team played in the 2016 Cal Ripken World Series, losing only in the U.S. Championship game to the team from my home state of Washington. The Go Nuts returned to the World Series again in 2017, this time falling just one game short of playing for the championship two years in a row!

If Principal Carganilla represents the heart of Farrington, it can be said that Farrington represents the heart and soul of the Kalihi neighborhood. Ever since New England missionary families first arrived in Hawaii in the early nineteenth century to work on Hawaii's sugar and pineapple plantations, they've needed a constant supply of cheap labor. And since the very beginning, the Kalihi neighborhood of Honolulu has been the first home to wave after wave of Chinese, Japanese, Korean, Philippine, Portuguese, Polynesian, and Micronesian laborers who first came to work in Hawaii's sugar cane mills and later the pineapple fields of the Dole Plantation. Today, Kalihi is still one of Honolulu's most ethnically diverse and poorest neighborhoods.

In Hawaiian, Kalihi means "the edge." It is a most appropriate name because the slopes of the Kalihi valley have been sharpened into a knife edge by the Kalihi stream flowing down to the Pacific Ocean from the Ko'olau Mountains. King Kamehameha V gave the area its name. The Kalihi stream is narrow and steep at the upper part until it spreads out lower down before it empties into the Honolulu Harbor.

When America engineered to overthrow the Hawaiian monarchy and seized control of Hawaii in 1905, Kalihi was still a residential district of Hawaiians and part-Hawaiians that attracted new arrivals with its cheaper cost of living. Later, as wave after wave of Japanese, Philippine, Portuguese, and other workers left the sugar plantations and mills, many of them settled in Kalihi.

In the first half of the twentieth century, Filipinos, Samoans, Koreans, and Southeast Asians followed. Cannery workers, dairy workers, farmers, schoolteachers, storekeepers, and others all lived and worked in Kalihi. In the 1920s and 1930s, these early residents were joined by others. Attracted by affordable housing and Kalihi's proximity to downtown Honolulu and U.S. military bases, many rented or purchased homes and commuted to work outside of Kalihi. Together with longtime residents, they continued to develop the neighborhood, adding churches, community organizations, and schools that created a unique blend of their distinctive cultures.

In its early days, Kalihi was a quiet, open area with gardens of every kind everywhere. Vegetable gardens, flower gardens, taro patches, grazing land, and chicken farms filled the valley. You could walk to any place you needed to go. But today, Kalihi is a dense, tightly packed urban setting. There's no empty space anymore, and the Farrington High School campus grounds make up the largest open area.

Still today, the Kalihi community attracts Hawaii's newest workers and their children, many of whom are now new immigrants from across the entire Pacific Rim, which includes hundreds of Micronesian islands, the Philippines, and Southeast Asia, islands we on the mainland have never heard of. These newer residents now occupy housing projects, rebuilt older homes, and newer single and multi-family dwellings.

Over the years, these waves of immigrants have built houses all the way up the valley. Their homes are now crowded tightly together right up to the mountains' knife-edge, where the land becomes too sharp and steep to build. Kalihi Elementary, one of the Farrington feeder schools we will learn more about later, sits tucked tightly up against the base of the mountains, at the valley's very narrowest point, and directly across the street from one of Hawaii's poorest Micronesian housing projects. Farrington High School lies a few miles down below in the dense, urban lower valley, along with a few of its other feeder schools: Kalihi Waena Elementary, Kalihi Uka Elementary, Kalihi Kai Elementary, King David Kalakaua Middle School, and Dole Middle School.

A Work in Progress

Farrington High School opened in 1936 and stands on Kalihi's southern ridge, just across the H1 Freeway from one of Hawaii's most famous historical treasures, the Bernice Pauahi Bishop Museum. It was named after Hawaii's first territorial governor, Wallace Rider Farrington, and students are known as the Governors. Today, with more than 2,400 students and 135 faculty,

Farrington High School has one of the largest student populations of all Hawaii's public schools. For the children of the waves of immigrants from the many countries and island cultures across the entire Pacific Rim, Farrington and its Kalihi feeder schools have been the gateway to America. I have found Farrington to be one of the most diverse and demographically challenged schools in all of America.

The ethnic diversity of Farrington is hard to imagine without living, working, or eating in Kalihi! If you enjoy testing your taste buds, there's an incredible variety of exciting food available in the neighborhood. Some of the tastiest can be found in the small mom-and-pop storefront shops and bakeries sprinkled throughout Kalihi. Sometimes, this tempting mixture of spices and flavors from around the world is creatively combined in delightful new ways. A faculty potluck at Farrington can be a foodie's delight!

It is the shared experience of living and working in this rich cultural and ethnic diversity of the Kalihi community that provides the colorful backdrop for the Farrington Way. And to really understand Farrington, you must first understand something about the history and culture of Kalihi and Hawaii. Because taken together, they form the foundation out of which Farrington's unique and highly collaborative school culture is being built.

To be clear, Farrington High School is not perfect. It is a work in progress. Culture is built every day from the collective relationships in a classroom or school. We choose our culture each day in the same way that we choose our attitude. Farrington simply chooses to put relationships and culture first. While not perfect, they are a model from which we can learn. What are some of the lessons?

Let's start with the obvious. Honolulu sits on Oahu, and Oahu is actually a very small island. You can easily drive completely around it in a single afternoon. Oahu is in the middle of the earth's largest ocean, and the Hawaiian Islands form the most remote archipelago, or string of islands, on our planet! That means they are the furthest away from any other land . . . 2,500 miles to be exact. In terms of today's travel on modern jet airliners, that doesn't seem so far.

But for most of Hawaii's history, each immigrant wave had to make the same difficult journey. After they managed to make what was most likely a hard trek to a seaport from which they could leave their home continent, they all had to spend what was often *months* in boats, relatively small boats, sailing across the world's largest body of water, to a teeny tiny speck of dry land in the middle of the Pacific Ocean.

This brief history lesson is important because it can help to understand something about what makes the culture of Hawaii so different. First, *every-*

one is an immigrant. Everyone came from somewhere else! The only difference is when they came. What we think of as "native" Hawaiians are the direct descendants of the ancient Polynesian voyagers who were the first to arrive more than a thousand years ago. They sailed thousands of miles across the open Pacific in outrigger canoes guided only by their concept of A'o about the stars, sea, and sun—a journey that was thought impossible by Europeans, who didn't make the voyage until over a century later.

Fire and Fury

Today's tropical paradise that we think of as Hawaii was born in fire and fury, a birthing process that is still under way, a process that you can still witness for yourself. On the morning of May 3, 2018, those on the Big Island of Hawaii got to see the Mt. Kilauea volcano up close, at the very moment when the Hawaiian Goddess Pele awoke! They watched in absolute awe as Pele began her most recent eruption, a violent event that eventually lasted for months and destroyed more than a thousand homes by burning and burying them in lava as Pele created new land that expanded the Big Island even further into the sea.

All of Hawaii was born like this, a barren volcanic rock in the middle of the Pacific Ocean. As we have seen, the string of islands we call Hawaii is the most remote land mass on earth. It took evolution more time to get started here. Almost all the trees, fruits, and flowers that we think of as Hawaiian were brought to Hawaii by those ancient Polynesian voyagers. It was their ancient concept of A'o that gave them the knowledge they needed to sail thousands of miles in open outrigger canoes. In a way, these ancient voyagers created much of the Hawaii we know today. They are the ones who brought the first coconut palms, the breadfruit, the taro, flowers, chickens, and pigs to Hawaii. It wasn't until much later, in the nineteenth century, that Europeans also added the sugar cane, pineapples, horses, and cattle.

Like the ocean's surf, wave after wave of immigrants came to Hawaii: Polynesian, American, European, Chinese, Japanese, Korean, Philippine, Portuguese, and Micronesian, all adding to what may be the most diverse cultural mix on the planet, all combined and confined on a tiny island in the middle of the Pacific Ocean. If you're ever lucky enough to explore these islands, you will find that people and places generally share a common respect for those ancient Polynesian voyagers who came first.

Evidence of that respect can be found as you travel across any Hawaiian island and you see brown roadside signs marking the location of ancient temples or shrines, known as a Heiau (hay-ow). These Heiau were a focal point for important aspects of ancient ceremonial life. If you look closely when visiting these Heiau, you will frequently find personal offerings left by visitors out of respect, and there are hundreds of Heiau (there is no plural form in the Hawaiian language) preserved throughout the state.

But maybe the strongest tribute paid to the Hawaiian culture is the fact that the Hawaiian language names, describes, and defines Hawaii to this day. It is a branch of the Austronesian language group that spreads over a wide triangle in the Pacific Ocean, from Hawaii in the center to New Zealand in the southwest and Easter Island to the east. While related, the languages in the group are not mutually intelligible today. But linguistic experts believe the genesis of the Hawaiian language dates from the arrival of Marquesan or Tahitian voyagers in Hawaii around 1000 CE.

The Aloha Spirit

Certainly, the most famous of all Hawaiian words is *Aloha*. It seems a simple word. Tourists find it fun using it to say both hello and goodbye. But like the concept of A'o, Aloha is easily misunderstood. Yes, Hawaiians do say Aloha when they meet or leave someone. But the greeting function of the word should not be taken literally. Like A'o, Aloha is simple on the surface but more complex as a holistic concept. The deeper, and more culturally complex, meaning of Aloha is that we have love, peace, and compassion for all we encounter.

The word *Aloha* can serve as a mantra, if you will—a constant reminder of how we should live our life, a life filled with the Aloha Spirit. To be filled

with the Aloha Spirit means our heart is so full of love, peace, and compassion that we have a positive influence on all those around us. To live our life filled with the Aloha Spirit is a worthy goal. Using the word *Aloha* can serve as a regular reminder of how we should treat those around us in the world. Understanding the A'o (teaching and learning) of Aloha means we can have a deeper appreciation of Hawaiian culture, one where family (Ohana) and positive relationships are so important.

It is important to remember that most Farrington students are not native Hawaiian and *Aloha* is not a word from one of the many languages spoken on campus. Native Hawaiian students and teachers make up a small minority. But all Farrington students are taught the concept of Aloha in the same way they are taught empathy and to celebrate their diversity. They are not asked to abandon the culture of their "home island" but to learn from all cultures, including their new home: Hawaii.

Hawaiians believe that the more you share the Aloha Spirit, the more it comes back to you. There are few places in Hawaii where the Aloha Spirit is stronger than at Farrington High School. The Farrington culture is being built purposefully on a foundation of positive relationships, a foundation where compassion and empathy are not left to chance but practiced with purpose, a foundation designed to connect and support every adult and student. And the Aloha Spirit serves as a mantra for all.

The Farrington culture also shares a common vision of rigorous and relevant learning for all, a culture of A'o, of teaching and learning for all. Through this shared vision, school leaders, teachers, and students are creating a highly effective learning school, a Model School, built on three things:

trust, empowerment, and collaboration. In part II of this book, we will explore ten specific strategies Farrington has used to earn teachers' trust and empower them to collaborate around their common vision of relationships, relevance, and rigor for all students and adults.

Farrington is building a learning culture based on A'o, the Hawaiian idea that teaching and learning are different sides of the same coin. Hawaiian language teacher Illiahi (Ilee-ah-hee) Doo explained to me that at Farrington everyone is teaching and learning. Teachers are learning from teachers; students are learning from students and teachers.

At Farrington teachers regularly collaborate to create some of the most rigorous, relevant, and interdisciplinary Quad D lessons ICLE has ever seen. These lessons not only connect classroom content to real-world problems, but they allow students to learn from teachers and industry professionals and also other students as well. To learn more about how this happens at Farrington, watch a short video, *Making Shift Happen in Hawaii*, at this YouTube link: youtu.be/RVuNY04ob6I.

Ma Ka Hana Ka Ike

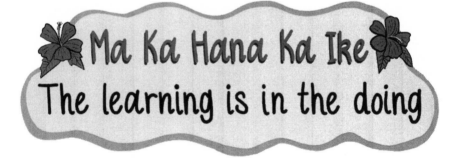

Dr. Bill Daggett's important insight, almost thirty years ago now, was that we learn rigorously best by application, not seeing, hearing, or even reading. We learn best by doing! That concept forms the vertical axis and the foundation of the Rigor/Relevance Framework. This idea resonates deeply in Hawaii. It was Auntie Verlie Ann Wright and Herb Lee of Hawaii's Kamehameha Foundation that first taught us the wisdom of this ancient concept in the Hawaiian language: Ma Ka Hana Ka Ike, which can be translated as the learning is in the doing. In other words, the secret to A'o is Ma Ka Hana Ka Ike = the secret to effective teaching and learning is in the doing![1]

But the Farrington Way means putting relationships first and into the proper scope and sequence: relationships, relevance, and rigor, in that order, please. The Farrington Way means that if you want better relationships, you must be intentional about building them. Being intentional about building relationships means you plan for better relationships; you budget and schedule for better relationships. And the Farrington Way means empathy and compassion are not left to chance. They are taught and modeled. There is no better evidence for this than the fact that in 2018 the Farrington student body chose special needs student Jasmine Cozo as their Homecoming Queen!

Jasmine was born with Down syndrome. But with the help of educational assistant Evelyn Utai and Farrington's FRIENDz Program, she didn't let that didn't stop her from becoming Homecoming Queen. After the Homecoming ceremony, Farrington quarterback Chris Afe said, "Everyone was excited. Her parents were excited. The school was excited." Homecoming King Jaymar Enanoria spoke for the entire student body when he said, "We choose to include and break barriers." Jasmine is well known and liked by her schoolmates. She is also a Special Olympics athlete, and last year Farrington High School was named a National Unified Champion School by Special Olympics.

At Farrington all means all, and that means all are included, regardless of the challenges they may face. Jasmine is a member of Farrington's award-winning FRIENDz Special Education Program, where special needs and general education students participate in all major school activities together. The FRIENDz Program is a prime example of what makes the Farrington school culture so special, and we will learn much more about it and the strategies they use in chapter 12.

What We Can Learn from Farrington

Many sociologists, psychologists, and political scientists believe our American culture is in crisis. The evidence is piling up around us that empathy is declining and the bonds of trust binding our society are breaking down. Neuroscientists and psychologists are sounding an alarm about the rapid decline of empathy, particularly in the young. Today's entering college freshmen are only half as empathetic as those in 2000, leading to what some scientists are calling a "crisis of narcissism."

What happens to a culture when empathy declines? What changes will occur in our culture if we lose the ability to empathize with each other? What will the decline of empathy mean for our schools, our students and teachers . . . our future? And finally, what can we learn from Model Schools like Farrington? These essential questions are at the heart of this book. Neuroscien-tists say that empathy is an essential ingredient for building trust. What is the relationship between the decline in empathy and the breakdown of trust in our American culture? What will this mean for our schools? We will explore these questions, and the research data they are producing, in chapter 4.

Finding answers to these questions will become increasingly important to every school leader and teacher. That is a big part of why this book was writ-ten. So, to be clear: there is something important and useful to be learned about building a positive culture from the strong relationships and trust found in the culture of the Farrington Way. Their ability to create a common vision that unites so many diverse cultures is something not only at which to marvel but from which to learn.

And we should not forget that Farrington is rooted deeply in the unique values and history of the Kalihi immigrant culture, and that the story of Kalihi may be the best way to understand the story of Hawaii, a tiny island where everyone came from somewhere else and found a way to get along. For sure, Hawaii's story has its share of sadness, dishonesty, destruction, and greed; those human failures are found everywhere, even in paradise. But to focus on them is not the Farrington Way.

At this dark and dangerous time in America's journey, we can all learn something valuable from Farrington and Hawaii. The truth is that the true beauty of Hawaii lies not in the land but in the hearts and spirit of its people. Palm trees are not required.

Note

1. See appendix A.

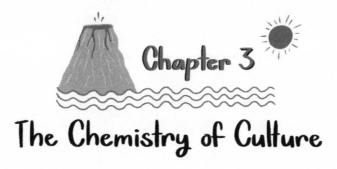

The Chemistry of Culture

You know you're a geek about teaching if there are few things you enjoy more than watching a great teacher and a class full of students passionately engaged in learning. There's an energy in the excitement of discovery that you can see and feel! It's easy to get hooked on that experience. And those of you who are hooked know that the culture of a classroom or school is very real—something you can most certainly see and feel.

The single most important element in building a positive, passionate, and engaging classroom culture is trust. Trust is not just important; it is essential. Trust is the foundation for everything else. No doubt about it, trust is a big deal. So hard to earn, so easy to lose. But just how do we decide to trust someone? We all know what trust feels like, and most of us have known that almost punch-to-the-gut feeling when it's broken with someone who matters. But how does that happen and what does it mean? Just what is trust? Where does it come from, and how does it start?

Is it possible that, as we go about our daily lives interacting with those around us, when we perceive another person as warm, caring, and competent, some type of "switch" in our brain gets turned on telling us that we can trust them? And when that trust gets broken, another "switch" gets thrown? It turns out that neuroscientists are learning that is exactly what happens. And a turning point in our understanding of trust was the discovery of the role the neurochemical called oxytocin plays in the process.

Trust Is a Drug

Neuroscientists are learning that, in fact, there is a chemistry of culture! And as they expand their exploration of how the brain works, they are also learning that the brain's chemistry creates the chemical foundation for our most basic human behaviors. And as these scientists are beginning to better understand the brain chemistry behind our relationships with others, they are learning that the human behavior and emotion we call trust is actually a drug, or more precisely a cocktail of drugs. And that this mysterious Chemistry of the Brain both governs, and is governed by, our relationships with others.

Even most of us non-scientists instinctively understand that our culture shapes our behavior and our behavior shapes our culture. But how does that happen? It seems to be some form of an intricate dance. What are the steps, and can we learn them? Until very recently, exactly how this is accomplished in our brain had largely remained a mystery. It is absolutely fascinating to learn how fast the field of cultural neuroscience has grown in just the past few years. And how, with new brain imaging techniques, neuroscientists around the world are now able to carry out absolutely amazing research that is unlocking previously hidden secrets about the inner workings of the human brain . . . and how it drives and determines our behavior—and the reverse . . . how behavior helps to "wire" our brain.

Neuroscience is generally defined as a branch (as neurophysiology) of science that deals with the anatomy, physiology, biochemistry, or molecular biology of nerves and nervous tissue and especially their relation to behavior and learning. We will say neuroscience follows the pathways of data flow within the CNS (central nervous system) and tries to define the kinds of processing going on there. And it uses that information to explain behavioral functions.

For the purposes of this book, the new field of cultural neuroscience specifically studies how culture can shape cognition, and vice versa. Neuroscientists study how our brains work in different situations and the relationships between culture, cognition, and brain function. Cultural neuroscience was made possible by the incredible rise of neuroimaging research techniques that allow us to see inside the brain as it is working and existing work in the field of cultural psychology.

OK, that's a lot of scientific terms. To be clear, this book is not written by a scientist and this is not a science book. The book's purpose is to examine the brain-based research behind the specific strategies you can use to increase the three essential elements required to build a more positive culture: trust, empowerment, and collaboration. To that end, the book will summarize neuroscience research in this chapter, and we will return to it as we explore each of the brain-based strategies in part II. For you science geeks (you know who you are) reading this who want more information, you will find references and links to this fascinating research throughout the book. (Am I revealing my own geekiness here?)

Your Brain on Trust

Let's start back in 2001 when neuroscientists Paul J. Zak and Steve Knack began to study the economic impact of trust in the business world. They asked these essential questions: Why do two people trust each other? And when they do, exactly what happens inside the brain? They hypothesized that there must be some signal, or "switch," in the brain that tells us when we should trust someone.

They knew from previous research in rodents that a brain chemical called oxytocin acted as a kind of signal when another animal was safe to approach. And they decided to measure the brain activity of people while they worked to see if it was also true in humans. They learned that when we interact positively with each other in a caring, empathetic, and ethical way, we also release oxytocin in our brains. Their studies eventually showed that the relationship between the amount of oxytocin produced and trustworthiness is so exact, it can actually be used to predict the level of trust in any relationship. Additional research has since shown that people given synthetic oxytocin are twice as likely to trust strangers and that it improves our connection to others by increasing our empathy.

We've all heard of the fight or flight impulse. But new brain research shows there is an equally powerful brain response when we positively interact with others. fMRI experiments have demonstrated that specific positive behaviors bathe brains in oxytocin, not only signaling us when the other person is safe and trustworthy but producing a significant reduction of brain activity in the areas associated with fear and stress.

Ultimately, Zak and Knack found that trust significantly improved the confidence in, and success of, business relationships, and their international study of forty-one countries showed trust was among the strongest predictors of business success.

You Never Get a Second Chance to Make a First Impression!

Psychologist Amy Cuddy has studied first impressions at Harvard Business School for more than fifteen years. She has discovered two key characteristics that predict how we "size up" another person: competence and warmth/

trustworthiness. Importantly, her work shows trustworthiness to be the single most important factor in how we judge and relate to others.

In a 2015 *Psychology Today* post, "The Neuroscience of Savoring Positive Emotions," Christopher Bergland reports that specific areas of the brain are activated in humans when receiving recognition and/or experiencing positive emotions. In general, people with more sustained levels of activity in these areas report higher levels of psychological well-being and have lower levels of the "stress hormone" cortisol.

But the brain is a complicated place, and scientists are still learning about oxytocin's interaction with other chemicals in the brain. It turns out the largely ladylike hormone estrogen increases a person's sensitivity to oxytocin, and multiple studies confirm that women release more oxytocin than men. Well, that explains a lot! Studies show that, in general, women connect more easily with others. Um . . . does that give them a leadership advantage?

Your Brain on Culture

"Your Brain on Culture" is a fascinating article written by Beth Azar that digs even deeper into the cultural differences in how our brains work. She explains that when an American man meets a stranger and thinks about whether the stranger is honest, his brain activity looks very different than when he's thinking about whether another person is honest, even a close relative. However, that's not true for Chinese people. When a Chinese man evaluates whether a stranger is honest, his brain activity looks almost identical to when he is thinking about whether his mother is honest.

The discovery that American and Chinese brains function differently when evaluating the relative trust of others suggests that people from collectivist cultures, such as China, think of themselves as deeply connected to other people in their lives, while Americans tend to show a strong sense of individuality. Neuroscience research has shown that the impact of culture even determines how our brains process information. A study by Yiyuan Tang of Dalian University of Technology in Dalian, China, found that Chinese and Americans actually do math differently. Chinese natives make use of different parts of the brain than Americans do when processing numbers.

Another study by Northwestern University psychologist Joan Chiao revealed that Chinese collectivist culture insulates against depression and that people from East Asian cultures are far more likely than Americans to have a gene that buffers them from depression.

Another cross-cultural study examined the well-known fact that American culture tends to reinforce dominant behavior and Japanese culture tends to reinforce subordinate behavior. In the study, American and Japanese subjects passively viewed visual stimuli related to dominance and subordination as neuroscientists measured neural responses and locations within the brain using fMRI. In Americans, the specific areas of the prefrontal cortex lit up when viewing dominant stimuli. These same areas responded in the Japanese when viewing subordinate stimuli.

In addition, Americans self-reported a tendency toward more dominant behavior whereas Japanese self-reported a tendency toward more subordinate behavior. The findings provided the first demonstration that culture can shape functional activity in the brain's mesolimbic reward system, which in turn may guide behavior.

Scientists are confirming that what the brain finds rewarding is determined by the values of the culture in which it finds itself. And that explains how different people can see the same thing but have completely different neural responses.

How Trust Creates Joy

According to Zak's research, "Experiments show that having a sense of higher purpose stimulates oxytocin production, as does trust. Trust and purpose then mutually reinforce each other, providing a mechanism for extended oxytocin release, which produces happiness."

Zak goes on to explain that our joy on the job comes from doing purpose-driven work with a trusted team. The correlation between (1) trust reinforced by purpose and (2) joy is very high: 0.77. "It means that joy can be considered a 'sufficient statistic' that reveals how effectively your culture engages employees. To measure this, simply ask, 'How much do you enjoy your job on a typical day?'"

Your Brain on Trust

Yes, you can "bathe brains" in oxytocin and when you do, you can measure the increase in joy and satisfaction your staff feels at work. The State of Hawaii requires all schools to collect what's called School Satisfaction

Survey (SQS) data each year. A table showing what this shift looks like over three years at Farrington High School and Kalihi Elementary School, its feeder, displays the steady growth in satisfaction over time across all groups.

Neuroscientists like Zak are confirming that the impact of culture on our brains is so strong that it can change the way we see the world. This helps explain the powerful impact of "mental models" on our behavior. The influence of mental models on how we see the teaching and learning, the A'o, in our classrooms is so strong that we will examine it separately and in much greater detail in chapter 5 and share a Culture Framework (mental model) that Farrington has found to be a useful guide for their work. In this chapter, we'll establish the underlying neuroscientific connection among how we see ourselves and the world, what's going on inside our brain, and the idea that our brain chemistry can be changed in dramatically different ways, depending upon our cultural values.

Tufts University psychologist Nalini Ambady has found that even when people see the same image, their brains may respond and process it very differently. In a study published in *Neuroimage*, researchers used MRIs to measure brain activity in American and Japanese subjects as they viewed silhouettes of bodies in postures considered "dominant" (for example, standing tall, arms crossed) and "submissive" (with head and arms hanging down).

The study was based on multiple studies showing that East Asian cultures value submissiveness, while Western cultures value dominance. They discovered not only that was this true, but that they could actually see this cultural distinction in the way the subjects' brains responded to visual input. When Americans viewed dominant silhouettes but not submissive ones, the brains' reward circuitry fired. But in the Japanese participants, the exact opposite was observed. Their brains' reward circuitry fired only in response to submissive images.

Even more interestingly, Ambady reported that the magnitude of the brain's response to these images correlated directly with the extent to which the Japanese and American subjects reported how much they valued dominance and submissiveness. The more a subject valued dominance, or being in control, the stronger their brain's reward circuitry fired when they viewed a dominant image. What this means is that what the brain finds rewarding reflects the values of its culture.

Neuroscientists are finding that cultures do actually see the world differently and that they can pick up this difference with brain imaging. Studies like these demonstrate that neuroscience can measure cultural differences and is changing the way scientists think about brain development. They're learning more about exactly how the chemistry of the brain can be changed by our culture and environment.

Using an analysis of the imaging data they developed in earlier studies, the researchers showed that Chinese participants' perceptual areas of the brain responded more to objects superimposed on incongruent scenes than objects matching their surroundings. This was not the case for Americans, who didn't appear to be affected by the background at all.

Recently, a study reported in *Social Cognitive and Affective Neuroscience* demonstrated that Westerners process human faces more actively than East Asians, consistent with the Western focus on individuality. Ambady concludes by saying, "East Asians and Americans literally see things differently—and that finding could have major implications for models of cross-cultural communication." Her studies suggest that seeing things differently may also help explain the observed differences in the ease with which different cultures perform the same cognitive tasks, such as studies showing that Americans pay more attention to details and Asians pay more attention to context. This research may help us understand why some cultures appear more skilled at certain real-life cognitive problems than others.

The Chemistry of A'o

ICLE has worked in Asia since its beginning. We have worked in Hawaii for ten years and extensively with Farrington High School in the Kalihi neighborhood of Honolulu. ICLE is grateful to them for their willingness to share their knowledge of A'o and culture.

Yes, Hawaii truly is that tropical paradise many of us dream about. Turquois seas, trade winds, and green-cloaked mountains have made many a picture postcard. But the geography is not what makes Hawaii unique. It is the culture!

The diversity of cultures in Hawaii is unlike anywhere else in America. The entire history of these islands is wave after wave of new cultures arriving from across the entire globe. These volcanic rocks in the middle of the Pacific produced no native culture. Everyone, and every culture, came as a wave arriving from some other shore, even the ancient Polynesian voyagers who came first.

This amazing cultural diversity must be experienced to be understood. It takes time, but observing the cultural differences on display here is incredibly fascinating. Hawaii makes the neuroscience of culture and the concept of A'o come alive. Here's the thing: Hawaii has managed to turn its greatest challenge—managing cultural diversity—into its greatest strength. This strength is an A'o so strong, and so important, all of America can learn from them today. That's another reason for this book.

This belief is supported by a growing body of neuroscientific research that clearly demonstrates the impact of culture on our brains and the cultural differences that brain chemicals can produce. Science helps us to understand how much the brain can be changed by our environment. The exciting part is that multiple studies now locate the exact areas and pathways of the brain involved in creating and sustaining positive emotions. These studies are showing exactly how the brain chemical oxytocin helps humans build trust, form friendships, and work well together on a team.

There is no longer any doubt that there is a "chemistry of culture" in our brain. Neuroscientists have confirmed the existence of specific chemicals that are activated by this neural network and their impact on how we interact and respond to other human beings around us. What can we learn from this brain science? We can learn that culture does not happen by chance, that a positive culture can be intentionally built. Neuroscience has shown there are specific leadership strategies that we can use to bathe brains in the right chemicals and that these strategies will build trust and improve relationships within any school. Conversely, in a toxic culture, there are management strategies that trigger the release of the wrong chemicals and have the exact opposite effect!

The brain research of Zak and others has identified specific leadership behaviors that increase oxytocin production in the brain and generate trust. Remember that John Hattie has identified the correlation between trust and joy as 0.77. This book will focus on six of the behaviors identified by neuroscience and we'll explore each of them briefly below. Each of the ten culture-building strategies described in part II of this book will be linked back to one or more of these leadership characteristics:

1. Show vulnerability.
2. Release control.
3. Create "challenge stress."
4. Recognize excellence.
5. Share information broadly.
6. Intentionally build relationships.

Behavior 1: Show Vulnerability
Being vulnerable means being open and honest about ourselves, most importantly about our mistakes and failures, and simply being able to say, "I don't know." Vulnerability is only found in high-trust organizations. Principals and teachers in high-trust schools can not only acknowledge their mistakes but

freely ask for help from colleagues. Paul Zak's research team found that this behavior stimulates oxytocin production and increases trust and cooperation. It is difficult to learn from others if we are not willing to admit what we don't know and to stop being the "expert." But I've observed that asking for help is a sign of a secure leader. Being open and honest about the things we do not know opens the door to new learning.

Behavior 2: Release Control

One reason so many principals and teachers are still the traditional "my way or the highway" kind of leaders is they fear losing accountability. That means we must learn strategies that allow us to release control without giving up accountability. We need to learn how to think about accountability in a new way. To successfully release control, we must learn how to create high but attainable goals and, most importantly, how to define more precisely what success looks like by establishing clear expectations . . . and then get out of the way!

Being trusted to figure things out is a big motivator. According to Paul Zak, a 2014 Citigroup and LinkedIn survey found that nearly half of employees would give up a 20 percent raise for greater control over how they work. Common sense tells us that when teachers and students are given more choices about which projects they'll work on and/or how they'll represent their work, their engagement and motivation increase. We will explore more about the idea of releasing control through one principal's specific strategy in chapter 7 of this book.

Behavior 3: Create "Challenge Stress"

Not all stress is created equal. When a teacher gives a student or group of students a difficult but achievable assignment, the stress of the task releases the neurochemicals oxytocin and adrenocorticotropin in the brain. These brain chemicals have been shown to help us focus and strengthen our social connections. When teachers must work together to complete a task, these same brain chemicals help coordinate their behaviors.

But this is only true if our assignments and tasks have well-defined expectations that are clearly understood and are believed to be achievable! In Paul Zak's words, "Vague or impossible goals cause people to give up before they even start." Good teachers understand that they need to closely monitor student progress and check for understanding frequently to make sure they are on track. The importance of perceived achievability is reinforced by findings from Harvard Business School professor Teresa Amabile about the power of progress. Professor Amabile analyzed twelve thousand diary entries of employees from a variety of companies, and she found that 76 percent of people reported that their best days involved making progress toward specific goals.

Behavior 4: Recognize Excellence

Many of you are thinking, "Wait just a darn minute . . . we've got this one covered! We recognize our people all the time!" Another way to say this is celebrate success. And, yes, we do see lots of school celebrations in schools, for both students and staff. But are you recognizing and celebrating in a way that releases the right chemistry of culture? Are you being strategic, intentional, thoughtful? Brain science says that how you do it matters. Because recognizing excellence, what Paul Zak also calls *Ovation*, explains a whopping 67 percent of any organization's trust!

Zak's brain research shows that "recognition has the largest effect on trust when it occurs immediately after a specific goal has been met, when it comes from peers, and when it's tangible, unexpected, personal, and public." Celebrating success publicly not only amplifies the release of oxytocin in our brains; it also inspires and encourages others around us. Highly effective cultures learn that when they do the celebration within a forum for sharing new ideas and best practices, it can provide more motivation for others to learn from them.

Behavior 5: Share Information Broadly

Nature abhors a vacuum, particularly when it comes to information. And when factual information is not available in any large organization, people will often resort to rumor and gossip. A 2015 study of 2.5 million manager-led teams in 195 countries found that employee engagement improved significantly when leaders had some form of daily communication with staff. And yet the same study found that only 40 percent of employees report that they are well informed about their organization's goals, strategies, and tactics.

Neuroscience says such uncertainty about expectations can lead to chronic stress, which inhibits the release of oxytocin and that undermines teamwork and effective collaboration. Transparent, open, and frequent communication is the solution. Principals that empower teachers, using some form of instructional leadership teams, to clearly define goals and outcomes and then broadly share those expectations reduce uncertainty and stress about where they are going.

Behavior 6: Intentionally Build Relationships

Neuroscientists have discovered that our brains have been hardwired by millions of years of human evolution to build relationships with other people, and the network of connections in your brain that oxytocin activates dates back to the dawn of our species. This network is ancient. We now know that our desire to trust, to form bonds with other human beings, is deeply embedded in our nature. But our species is also very goal- and task-oriented. As a result, we sometimes fail to understand the importance of making the time to build relationships.

Yet brain research from Paul Zak's lab has shown that when people do make the time to *intentionally* build relationships on the job, both their performance and work satisfaction improve. Another study of software engineers in Silicon Valley found that "those who connected with others and helped them with their projects not only earned the respect and trust of their peers but were also more productive themselves."

And here's one more important reason we all need to be more intentional about building relationships: the decline of empathy! In our next chapter, we will explore the dramatic decline of empathy in our culture; ongoing research shows that empathy in college students has declined a jaw-dropping 40 percent since 2000! And studies show it's not just college students; empathy is declining across all demographic groups in our country, and the rate of that decline is rapidly accelerating! This is such a serious challenge to our culture that we will devote the entire next chapter to exploring what this loss of empathy means for the future of our children, our culture, and our country.

But the good news is that there are many things we can do to build better relationships. The culture-building strategies in part II of this book are based on the latest brain research and have been proven to work. These strategies show that you *can* help your teachers and students build better relationships in many ways. And there is hard science to say that when a team cares about one another, they perform better. The brain research findings show clearly that better relationships = more empathy, and more empathy = greater trust. And trust is the foundation of your school or classroom culture.

Trust, Collaboration, and Empowerment Are Connected

What exactly does this all mean? Taken together, these studies connect the chemistry of our brains to our daily actions and interactions. They dramatically highlight the importance of trust in building a positive culture. They show that our desire and ability to trust each other has been hardwired into our DNA by millions of years of evolution, that our ability to work together has played an important role in the survival of our species, and that building trust with each other is ultimately in the best interest of all of us.

However, these studies also point to a serious downside. Our desire and instinct to trust is so strong it can, and often does, override our prefrontal cortex where logic and reason reside. It can even cause us to act against our own self-interest. The con men among us instinctively understand this. They become experts in fooling others into trusting them. They use the chemistry of culture for their own selfish purpose.

But let's bring this back down to earth, or at least to the classroom. What does the science say to our schools? And how do we connect these discoveries to the daily actions and interactions in our schools and classrooms? Our first big takeaway is the absolute importance of trust in school culture. Most of us have instinctively known this for some time. ICLE has come to better understand it by closely observing and reflecting on two different kinds of schools: the hundreds of struggling, or turn-around, schools they've worked with over the years, compared to ICLE's Model Schools.

ICLE has learned you can explain the difference between these two groups of schools, with one word: *trust*. If you want to explain as succinctly as possible how a school makes the journey from struggling to so successful they become a model for others to follow, it is *trust*. Certainly, there are many other essential steps on this journey. But the absolute non-negotiable, foundational, first step is: trust. You will not find an exception to this rule. You. Must. Build. Trust.

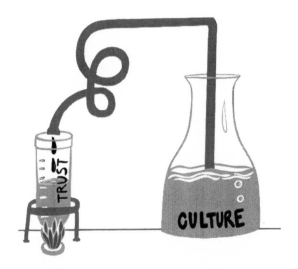

The neuroscience says that your staff's desire and ability to trust each other has been hardwired into their DNA by human evolution. By better understanding the chemistry of culture, we can improve our ability to collaborate and to empower each other. Part II of this book will help you bring this research out of the lab and into your school. You will learn how you can use specific strategies to bathe your staff's brains in the neurochemicals needed to build trust in any school or classroom. These strategies will add many links to our circle of A'o and connect the modern discoveries in neuroscience with the wisdom of the ancient Hawaiian voyaging culture that is several thousands of years old.

What does the science say that we can use in our schools? The challenge for school leaders and teachers is to build a school and classroom culture where the brain chemical oxytocin can be released many times during the school day. By better understanding just how oxytocin activates the brain, you can intentionally plan to create more opportunities for oxytocin to help you build trust between everyone—administrators, teachers, students, parents, and community.

If you've read this far, you're probably already thinking about the culture of your own school or classroom. And, yes, most of you have seen that, given time, trust can begin to build on its own. But one takeaway from the neuroscience research is that in highly effective cultures, leaders understand that trust is too important to be left to chance. So they don't!

At the core of this book is the idea that we should be intentional about building trust, that there are specific leadership strategies and characteristics that research shows have a significant and measurable impact on culture, and that we should think strategically about building trust. That means we should plan for building trust, budget for building trust, and monitor trust to make sure our plan is successful.

In part II of this book, we will explore specific brain-based strategies you can begin using today to build a better culture. Each of these strategies are based on our current understanding of the chemistry of culture. In part II, will explore each of these strategies in detail and the brain-based research that supports them.

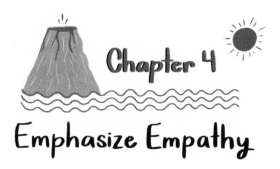

Emphasize Empathy

Empathy in college students has declined over 40 percent since 2000! Think about that for a minute. This finding, from a study of empathy in more than fourteen thousand college students by University of Michigan researchers, caused quite a stir when it was presented to the annual meeting of the Association for Psychological Science and reported in *Psychology Today*. The study showed that students starting college after 2000 have empathy levels that are *40 percent lower* than those who came before them.

And it's happening at every level. New research into bullying from the University of Kansas showed that measures of cognitive empathy in students transitioning to middle school also show evidence of significant decline. Cognitive empathy is defined as the ability to take another person's perspective into consideration. Remarkably, empathy declined whether the students had displayed bullying behaviors or had been the victims of them.

Even a quick review of the literature will turn up multiple studies that show the decline of empathy across different demographic groups. In our culture as a whole, empathy has declined 48 percent in the thirty years between 1979 and 2009. These are not isolated studies. Google "empathy" for yourself. Not only is empathy dramatically declining in our culture, but the *rate of the decline* is actually accelerating in young people. You'll also learn that there are things we can do about it.

Research into declining empathy done by psychologist Jean Twenge has led her to conclude that we are experiencing what she has called a "Narcissism Epidemic." Her research found increasing numbers of students

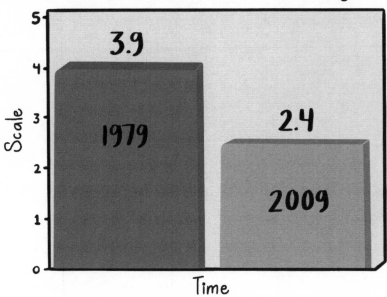

The Decline of Empathy

exhibiting personality traits leading to a diagnosis of narcissistic personality disorder, an extreme condition that arises when people are so self-absorbed that other people are seen only as objects to reflect their glory.

Would you like to test your empathy level against today's college students? You can do so by taking the University of Michigan's Empathy Survey at this link: umich.qualtrics.com/jfe/form/SV_bCvraMmZBCcov52?SVI=&Q_JFE=qdg.

In our work with schools and districts across the country, ICLE has certainly found this issue rising to the top of many educators' radar screens. It is often paired with the related problem of bullying. Lack of empathy is also resonating in our national media and political conversations. In his memorial speech following the January 2011 mass shooting in Tucson, Arizona, President Obama called on us to "sharpen our instincts for empathy." These studies suggest we may have a lot of work to do.

But as concerning as these findings are, the research also holds out hope. The University of Kansas middle school study concluded that you can increase empathy in children by focusing on improving social-emotional skills such as cognitive empathy, friendship development, and conflict resolution. By effectively teaching these social-emotional skills in elementary grades, we can help prevent bullying behavior before students enter middle school, when research has long shown bullying behavior generally increases. Many middle school teachers or principals confirm what the research is saying: that this is a growing problem in middle school.

～

Empathy = the ability to understand and share the feelings of another

～

What Happens When Empathy Declines?

Psychologists have long recognized the importance of empathy. It is considered one of the primary characteristics that help to define us as human. Created in 1943, the Heider-Simmel Test is one of the longest-running, consistently administered psychological tests of empathy.

The Heider-Simmel Test consists of having subjects watch a short, ninety-second animated video (the original was a stop-motion cartoon) and then take a short questionnaire designed to measure their empathetic response. It is fascinating and revealing. There are several versions of this classic test you can take for yourself online, like this one on Vimeo: youtube/ BUXMK_xR9XE.

There are multiple sources for interpreting your Heider-Simmel Results, like this one: musingsofanaspie.com/2014/04/08/interpreting-the-heider -simmel-animation/.

The Heider-Simmel is only one of many tests used to measure empathy in humans. What social scientists find alarming is that the decline of empathy, and the accelerating rate of its decline, is consistent across almost all of their different measures. Clearly, something significant is changing in our culture.

How empathetic are you? Want to measure and track your own empathy over time? There are a number of excellent free surveys available online, such as this Empathy Quiz from the Greater Good Science Center at UC Berkley: greatergood.berkeley.edu/quizzes/take_quiz/empathy.

The decline of empathy is igniting an explosion of new research and discussion among social scientists and neuroscientists. They are beginning to ask: why is empathy declining? What is changing in our culture to cause these dramatic changes in our children? What can our society do about it?

Increasingly we find that teachers and school leaders are quick to recognize the reality of this trend. They see it firsthand every day. One of the easiest ways to get any group of teachers affirmatively nodding their heads is to say something like "today's young people are 'wired differently.'" But what does that mean? Here are a few essential questions that we will explore together in this book:

1. What happens to a culture when empathy declines?
2. What changes in a culture as we lose our ability to empathize with each other?
3. What will this decline mean for our schools, our teachers, and our students?
4. What can we learn from Model Schools like Farrington High School?

The reality is scientists still don't have hard answers to these questions yet, largely because there are fewer research studies designed to examine the reasons why empathy is declining. But many educators are already asking themselves these questions because so many of them are on the front lines of this problem. And many educators have started to form their own ideas about why and often have good suggestions for future research.

Certainly, technology is a prime suspect. The growing pervasiveness of technology in all our lives must surely have some impact. What about the social media platforms so many of us have become almost addicted to? We use those apps because they are designed to connect us. But could they actually be creating *more* distance between us? How is that possible? And, of course, what role does the violence in video games and electronic media play? The reality is that there is much work to do before we can even begin to answer these questions, and it may be best to leave that discussion for another time.

Why the Decline in Empathy Matters

The word *empathy* has recently been cited so often for making a difference at work and in society that it was one of Merriam-Webster's top four words of 2017. And like much of the brain research on empathy, culture, and relationships, the question of *why* empathy is so important is being driven by the business world. Empathy has entered today's business vocabulary and social awareness in a big way for one reason: business has discovered the direct impact empathy has on their bottom line.

Businessolver's 2017 Workplace Empathy Monitor found that empathy has a direct impact on the bottom line by directly impacting employee productivity, loyalty, and engagement. Highlights from their 2017 report include:

- Eighty-seven percent of CEOs and 79 percent of HR professionals believe a company's financial performance is tied to empathy in the workplace.
- Eighty percent of all employees agree an empathetic workplace has a positive impact on business performance, motivates workers, and increases productivity.
- Ninety-two percent of employees believe empathy is undervalued.
- Seventy-seven percent of employees would be willing to work *more* hours for a more empathetic workplace, and 60 percent would actually accept a slashed salary for the same.
- Ninety-two percent of HR professionals say a compassionate workplace is a major factor in employee retention.
- Eighty percent of millennials noted that they would leave their current job if their office became less empathetic. Sixty-six percent of baby boomers also shared this sentiment.
- Yet less than *50 percent of employees* rate their workplaces as empathetic.

You can read the full report and take the survey yourself at: www.businessolver.com/resources/businessolver-empathy-monitor.

Why is business leading this conversation? Because they've come to understand that if empathy is the ability to understand and experience the feelings of another, then demonstrating empathy draws people together. Empathy creates a personal connection. And this is important: personal connections are more important than ever as trust in our institutions, media, and government is at an all-time low.

The word *empathy* was named one of Merriam-Webster's top four words of 2017.

We are learning there's just not a big difference between the business world and education in how they approach empathy. As both worlds race faster and faster to keep pace with the increasing pressures of accountability and technological change, empathy can easily fall out of fashion. Too often empathy is seen as something nice but something sort of soft and fuzzy. After all, we don't really test for that, do we? Instructional coaches at ICLE often have teachers complain about feeling overwhelmed by technology or the top-down pressure of testing. As one excellent teacher told us, he was tired of feeling like an "accountability zombie."

The most recent Gallup Organization's State of the Global Workplace Survey shows that only 31 percent of U.S. employees feel engaged at work. Further, Gallup found that high-performing employees who are not engaged are just as likely to leave an organization as those who have performance issues. Many social scientists who study the issue are convinced there's a growing number of workers—teachers and business employees—who believe that empathy is lacking in their organizations. Business leaders are sometimes finding out the hard way what surveys show: some of their best employees are willing to leave their jobs to find more empathetic employers!

What Does All This Mean for Schools?

What can our schools learn from the business world if we want to keep our best and brightest teachers? We must begin to understand that, like trust, empathy is one of the essential foundations of an effective culture—that an empathetic school is a school that recognizes and helps teachers achieve their professional goals, career needs, and personal priorities outside of school—in other words, the whole person. To put it simply, we must emphasize and exercise empathy. In part II of this book, we will examine specific strategies to do just that.[1]

The hard truth is that for the past two decades many of the major educational trends impacting our schools have been moving us away from the idea of creating a culture that nurtures empathy. The relentless focus on testing, data, and accountability, while arguably necessary and well-intended, too often meant there was little time left over for culture or relationship building.

As school leaders, we must face the fact that the measurable declines in the soft skills like empathy and social, emotional, and interpersonal skills are not just confined to our students. They are having an equal impact on the younger teachers and administrators entering our profession. These declines are real. And they will not reverse themselves. We must take action.

The rapid increase of instructional technology in our classrooms and schools brings with it another significant challenge. All across the country many educators have pushed for more, faster integration of technology for the past twenty years, while at the same time, more teachers are seeing, and thinking about, its negative impact on their students and classroom culture. The supporters of ideas like blended learning are growing. But as ICLE Senior Fellow Wes Kieschnick reminds us in his book, *Bold School*, "Technology is awesome. Teachers are better!"

In chapter 13, you will meet Sean Witwer, a special education teacher who has been following Wes Kieschnick's *Bold School* lead by using a blended learning strategy that allows him to leverage technology to deliver personalized instruction. By using computers, he can deliver course content through direct instruction and differentiate according to each student's individual needs. Mr. Witwer has totally transitioned from being the "sage on the stage" to a "guide on the side" and empowered students with greater responsibility for their own learning by having more time to build better relationships.

Individual teachers have been experimenting with different forms of the "flipped class" model for years. Master flippers, like Bozeman High School's Paul Andersen, have achieved remarkable success. Paul totally re-invented his science classroom, raised test scores, and was named Montana's Teacher of the Year. Paul did what so many educators dream about: using game theory, he turned his own science class into a video game!

But it is difficult to see how empathy can develop in a pure online learning environment, absent some form of a student-teacher relationship. This does not mean that students will learn content less or that technology can't be a teacher's most useful tool. But at what cost to our students' interpersonal skills and emotional intelligence? We need much more research to fully understand what is lost when our students learn online. Are we directly contributing to the decline of empathy? And if the culture surrounding us does in fact shape our brain's capacity for trust, then we need to be providing our students and schools with as many opportunities as possible for exercising empathy.

In Farrington High School's culture of A'o, everyone is teaching and learning. Teachers learn from teachers, students learn from students and teachers, and teachers regularly collaborate to create interdisciplinary, real-world lessons. At Farrington, teachers have the autonomy to experiment freely without fear of failure. They are entrusted to lead professional learning for their peers because administrators trust teachers to know their students best and have the experience, expertise, and heart to move the school forward.

Farrington is a Model School because they've created a "learning culture" where everyone is both teaching and learning. This is a culture that has chosen to emphasize empathy, a culture where every professional development session begins with empathy exercises where teachers build relationships and practice reading body language, hearing voices, making eye contact, and reading facial expressions. At Farrington they do not leave empathy to chance.

When you show deep empathy toward others, their defensive energy goes down, and positive energy replaces it. That's when you can get more creative in solving problems.

—Stephen Covey

There is no better evidence for Farrington's commitment to emphasizing and exercising empathy than their annual May Day Celebration, which they celebrate as Founder's Day in honor of Governor Wallace Rider Farrington, the school's namesake, whose birthday is May 3.

To celebrate May Day, all the cultural groups that make up the student body—the Hawaiians, Filipinos, Samoan, Tongan, Micronesian, Japanese, Chinese, Korean, Portuguese, Marshallese, and more—dance. The students dress in clothes from their native culture and perform a traditional dance from their home.

May Day at Farrington is an incredibly exciting experience. But what makes this show special is the audience response. It is not a competition. It is a celebration, a celebration of their diversity. There are no winners and losers. Every group is cheered and supported in a way you will seldom see anywhere on the mainland. In the appendix, you will find multiple links to videos so that you may see this celebration of diversity for yourself. Sadly, Farrington seems to be an exception to the trends in our society.

We Can Make Schools More Empathetic

There is a strong consensus among scientists that empathy is declining in our contemporary culture and most particularly in the young. At the same time, research in fields such as neuroscience, primatology, psychology, and social psychology is clearly demonstrating that while competition is innate to humans, so is empathy. We learned in chapter 3 that neuroscience says our desire and ability to trust each other have been hardwired into our DNA by human evolution. By better understanding the brain chemistry of culture building, you can improve your school's ability to collaborate and to empower each other. From Farrington High School, we will learn ways to do this.

In chapter 3 we also learned that neuroscientists like Paul Zak are confirming how our school's culture (relationships) changes the chemicals in our brain. Scientists are learning that the brain's chemistry creates the chemical foundation for our outward behaviors. And as they better understand the brain chemistry behind our relationships, they are learning how our culture creates a cocktail of drugs in our brains and, like a delicate dance, the chemistry of our brain both governs, and is governed by, our culture.

At ICLE, one of the lessons we've learned from schools who have made the journey from struggling to successful is: if your culture is broken, you can't fix anything else! We've observed over and over again that what matters most in a successful school is the culture. If that culture lacks trust and promotes competition, then our brains become wired to prioritize competition. If that culture promotes empathy, cooperation, and collaboration, more positive chemicals like oxytocin are released in our brains, and trust grows.

What we've learned from research in both the field of neuroscience and from Farrington High School is that we are indeed capable of creating a better, more humane, and more empathic culture than we currently have. These lessons are cause for hope. Because empathy impacts far more than our personal relationships, it shapes the way we see and experience the world around us and how we interact with others who share our space. At a time when empathy is rising to the top of so many radar screens, it's more important than ever to understand the practical applications of empathy in daily life and how to increase empathy in our classrooms and schools.

In chapter 2, we learned that Farrington High School is one school that does exactly that. Farrington's positive culture is built on three things: trust, collaboration, and empowerment. Empathy is the grease that lubricates our relationships. And in chapter 3, we learned how Farrington's positive culture literally bathes brains in good chemicals like oxytocin.

In part II of this book, from Farrington and its feeder schools, we will learn specific strategies they use to build empathy regularly. But first, let's explore three guiding principles that anyone can use to become more empathetic.

1. Practice Self-Empathy

Social scientists seem to agree that one of the biggest reasons empathy has declined is simply because we don't practice it as much anymore. We often spend more time with screens today than we do people. But the good news is that you absolutely *can* create a more empathic classroom or school culture. All you've got to do is practice it. Really. It's that simple. And fun.

You don't have to give up screens (or ask your students to!). It's not either/or. It's all about balance. Anyone can learn how to improve empathy skills with a little practice and time. And the more you practice and become comfortable with your students or staff, the more enjoyable and the more fun it becomes. Remember, our brains are hardwired by millions of years of evolution to build relationships.

Try not to let one negative experience or a single toxic coworker keep you from practicing a positive outlook. Remember, our feelings follow our thoughts, not the other way around. Feelings follow thoughts, behaviors follow feelings, and our behaviors create our culture. Start by practicing taking charge of your thoughts. And we can do that by practicing self-empathy. Take charge of the thoughts whizzing through your head. (See more exercises in chapter 11 for that.) Monitoring and managing the thoughts in your head will lead to more positive thoughts and start you on the road to emphasizing empathy.

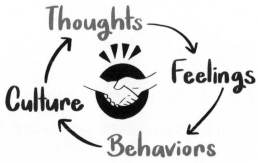

The Culture Cycle

2. Practice Empathetic Listening

Have you ever been locked in a serious conversation and suddenly become aware that the other person was not hearing you at all? Maybe it was because they weren't listening, because instead of listening to what you were saying, they were only thinking about what *they* would say next. *Question: do you ever do the same thing?* You see, listening and hearing are two different things. To hear and understand, we must practice.

Read each descriptor below and reflect on examples from your own personal listening experience:

- *Distracted Listening* happens when we are so distracted by other things that we are not really listening (or hearing) the other person at all. For example, a student is speaking to us, but we are focused on the conversation of a group of students in the corner of the room.
- *Pretend Listening* happens when we are at least making an effort to give the impression that we are listening. For example, while a student is speaking to us we may be saying, "I see" or "OK" as they are talking, but we are actually focused on reading an e-mail.
- *Selective Listening* happens most often when a colleague is talking to us and we are so busy figuring out what we want to say next that we're not thinking about what they are saying to us in that moment, or when a colleague is speaking to us but we are only listening for things we want to hear or already agree with. We switch off when another teacher starts talking about something we find uninteresting or jump to a conclusion about what they're saying instead of understanding what they are really saying; or instead of concentrating on what they are saying, we are thinking about how we will reply and whether we agree or not.

Empathetic Listening is the most difficult level of listening. It requires for us to affirmatively respond to what is being said, while it is being said—not that we agree, but that we are hearing. For example, making eye contact and nodding are some immediate signs we are thinking about what we are hearing. More difficult still, we must try to remove our own perspective from the conversation, put ourselves in the other person's shoes, and listen to the other person from their perspective. An example would be when a parent is calling about an issue that is familiar to you: you can understand how unfamiliar and confusing the issue might be to them by listening close enough to what they're saying to see the problem through their eyes.

3. Practice Asking Empathetic Questions

As teachers, we like to think we're masters of the art of questioning. But exercising empathy with our colleagues and students means not only being an empathetic listener but also asking empathetic questions in order to better understand our colleagues' or students' problems. When you ask empathetic questions, you're not just saying, "I hear you" but "I can understand the problem from your perspective, and what can I do to help?" Empathetic questions asked of colleagues and students should be specific rather than a one-size-fits-all response. Your colleagues and students deserve to have their concerns heard and understood.

Farrington High School has learned that empathy is a skill that can be built and improved over time. But if you want it to improve, you must work on it. Below are four strategies they used to guide their work as they planned to improve their culture.

P-L-A-N to Expand Empathy

1. Prioritize
   Make empathy a leadership focus. Include empathy in your action planning. Plan for it, budget for it, schedule for it. There are activities and exercises available in chapter 11 and in the appendixes that you can use. But learning empathy, like learning any skill, needs to include practice and expert feedback over time.

2. Learn to Balance
   In both your classroom and school, balance digital and face-to-face communications. Make time to talk. You don't have to stop texting, but make time to talk. Consider a no-tech policy during some meetings that includes time when mobile phones/laptop are not to be used. You'll find an amazing difference in attention and dialogue. Face-to-face conversations require the ability to listen, make eye contact, and encourage feedback without hiding behind a text message. Research and use a blended learning model for technology in the classroom. Remember, technology is awesome. Teachers are better!

3. Assess It Regularly
   Assess the level of empathy in your classroom or school using a variety of surveys and free tools available online. Keep track of the data over time. Is empathy getting better or worse? Survey for specifics about quality of day-to-day interactions using a School Climate Survey. Self-empathy is a starting point for improving empathy. Seeking feedback on empathy from an empathy coach should be encouraged.

4. Never Stop Looking for New Ways
   Never stop looking for new and creative ways to become more empathetic. Farrington High School's weekly teacher-led PD sessions always start with activities designed to build better relationships and increase empathy. How can you find time in your classroom or school schedule?[2]

Notes

1. Empathy exercise links:
   8 Steps to Create Empathy at School: www.askspoke.com/blog/support/work place-empathy/
   5 Empathy Exercises: www.livechat100.com/blog/empathy-training-activities
   The Mirror Exercise: www.youtube.com/watch?v=w13LC6DLMn8
   Exercises for Your Classroom: www.oakland.edu/Assets/Oakland/galileo/files-and -documents/Empathy%20in%20Your%20Classroom%20Teachers%20Guild. pdf.
2. See appendix B.

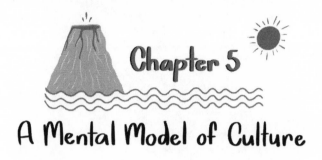

A Mental Model of Culture

Why Are Mental Models So Important?

Improving school culture really is a journey, a never-ending one. And when setting out on any journey to a place we've never been before, the first thing we need is a good map. A good map is not just nice to have—it is essential. That's exactly what a mental model is: a good map. Without a good map, you don't know where you're going, you don't know what the destination looks like, you won't know when you arrive . . . and you can easily get lost!

Just why are mental models so important? Because, like the prisoners in Plato's cave, very few of us are able to see the world as it actually is. Artists, mystics, poets, they catch glimpses. The rest of us see only shadows . . . and what our mental model of reality allows us to see.

The teachers and principals who most effectively increase the rigor and relevance in their schools have learned that the first and most important thing they need before beginning their journey is a new mental model of what a "good" teacher is. That new model should include a flexible framework to guide their journey, a framework they can use as a map to make decisions while moving forward.

What teachers and principals often need most is not more initiatives, programs, or tools but better mental models to help them think more strategically about using the tools they already have. Dr. Richard Jones describes it this way: "A mental model is an internal symbol or representation of external reality. The right mental model is like having a map to a city. Professional development in mental models introduces a framework, gives concrete ex-

amples, and encourages patterns of reflective thought and conversations to act consistently in these mental models."

Finding our way in the world today has become much easier since we added the GPS (global positioning system). A GPS instrument provides us a well-marked map. It also has the exact position of where we are on the route to our destination. This convenient technology has made it much easier to find our way in unknown territory.

When we hike familiar trails, we know the route and can enjoy the experience without worrying about getting lost or reading a map. This comfortable experience of hiking can be compared to the conditions in many schools, where a culture of focusing on preparing students for the next grade level, hopefully moving on to college, and so on is familiar territory for educators, who can continue following their comfortable route and enjoy the experience. However, when we introduce any new program or initiative, that comfortable route takes on a very different experience, and educators, like hikers, can find themselves uncomfortable in uncharted territory. The environment around them is unfamiliar. They can become unsure of their destination, even lost. They desperately need a map.

Creating real change in schools is a fluid process. Just like every student, every school has its own unique DNA. There is no single detailed blueprint to follow for success, no one path that works best for everyone. However, there most certainly are lessons that can be learned from other schools. Dr. Bill Daggett has worked with schools and districts across the country for more than twenty-five years to share best practices, conduct research, and support school leaders in facilitating changes that lead to measurable improvement. He says with some certainty that "changing mental models is one of the most important first steps."

In this chapter, we will explore three different but related mental models for schools. The first is the foundational Rigor/Relevance Framework focused on the teacher and effective instructional delivery in the classroom. Then we will examine the Leadership Framework and how it can be used by school leaders as a guide for reflection on the dynamic process of leading teachers in their instructional practice.

Finally, we will introduce the Culture Framework.[1] This model can help us better understand the current chemistry of the culture in our classrooms and schools and what we must do to improve it. By applying the Culture Framework, we will learn how it can be used to change a compliant culture into one that is committed and innovative. To do that, we will apply all that we have learned in earlier chapters about the power of trust to build better relationships, empower each other, and improve our ability to collaborate more effectively.

Let's begin at the beginning. For more than twenty-five years, thousands of principals and teachers have found the Rigor/Relevance Framework to be one of their most effective mental models for creating effective instruction. It never fails to help them locate "True North" in their classroom. They have learned how it can serve as a reliable guide in preparing students for success on new state standards and assessments like the Smarter Balanced Assessment.

The Rigor/Relevance Framework

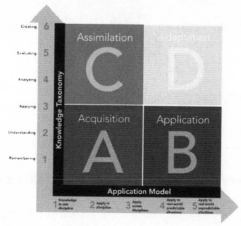

The Rigor/Relevance Framework is a matrix.[2] You can plot points along each axis that can be used to divide the framework into four quadrants. The Knowledge Taxonomy forms a continuum along the vertical axis based on the six levels of Bloom's Taxonomy, which describes the increasingly complex ways in which we think. The low end involves acquiring knowledge and being able to recall or locate that knowledge. The high end labels the more complex ways in which individuals use knowledge, such as taking several pieces of knowledge and combining them in both logical and creative ways.

The second continuum, known as the Application Model, forms the horizontal axis. It is one of action or, as they understand in Hawaii, Ma Ka Hana Ka Ike . . . learning by doing. Its five levels each describe putting knowledge to use. While the low end is knowledge acquired for its own sake, the high end signifies how we can use that knowledge to solve complex real-world problems and to create unique projects, designs, and other works for use in real-world situations.

The Rigor/Relevance Framework forms a matrix we can use to plot four quadrants. Each quadrant is labeled with a term that characterizes the learning or student performance at that level. The Rigor/Relevance Framework is an easy-to-understand map of effective instruction. With its simple, straightforward structure, it can serve as a bridge between school and the community. It offers a common language with which to express the notion of a more rigorous and relevant curriculum.

The Leadership Framework

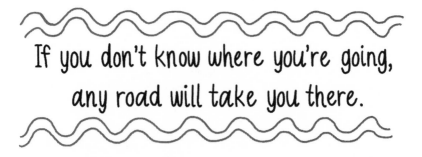

If you don't know where you're going, any road will take you there.

But Dr. Jones also recognized that school leadership is a fluid, dynamic process. Leaders must deal daily with constant challenges while keeping the school moving forward toward the goal of improved student outcomes. That means, in addition to a deep understanding of instructional delivery, school leaders also need a mental model to guide the process of school leadership. He decided to extend the original matrix concept of the Rigor/Relevance Framework into a new framework that leaders can use to describe and understand effective leadership.

The Leadership Framework allows leaders to draw upon their talents and experience to lead a school community, while continually reflecting on decisions and actions that optimize student learning. What benefits school leaders the most is not so much a list of good leadership practices but a mental model, or map, that helps them in decision making and problem solving.

The Leadership Framework is an effective blending of vision and empowerment that describes an adaptive process by which leaders, staff, and students take action to improve teaching and learning in their school. Dr. Jones's idea of Quadrant D leadership is an outgrowth of the research the International Center has done on school leadership through its extensive work with Model Schools across the country. In working closely with thousands of schools in hundreds of districts, ICLE has learned a great deal about the leadership skills that yield the best results. The Quadrant D Leadership Framework applies that learning.

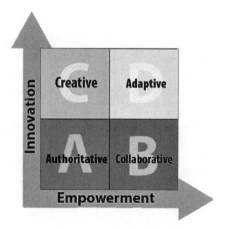

Quadrant D Leadership

Like the Rigor/Relevance Framework, the Leadership Framework can be divided into four quadrants and labeled along a vertical knowledge continuum and a horizontal application continuum. To reach higher levels of knowledge, you must raise the level of thinking about what is important in a school. At a low level of knowledge, leaders acquire understanding of school practices and the management of day-to-day tasks.

The application of leadership is on the horizontal continuum. At lower levels, leadership is most often defined by position and traditional command-and-control practices. Decision making is positional with problems being solved in isolation. At higher levels on the application continuum, leadership shifts from the actions of a single leader to a variety of leadership teams. Greater empowerment increases the distribution of leadership from a single leader to an entire school community taking leadership actions.

The Four Quadrants of the Leadership Framework

Leadership in Quadrant A (Authoritative Leadership) applies to traditional leaders, such as the principal, assistant principals, and department chairpersons, acquiring the skills they need and making decisions independently with respect to school improvement and student achievement. Usually, the Quadrant A leader decides and others act. Roles often labeled as "manager" would apply here.

Leadership in Quadrant B (Collaborative Leadership) involves the application of leadership not just by traditional leaders but also by staff. Actions are not based on submitting a problem to a higher level of authority and waiting for a decision. All staff, and ultimately students, work in a highly collaborative environment and take action consistent with the school goals.

Leadership in Quadrant C (Creative Leadership) characterizes higher-level thinking in which leaders are more reflective and innovative. They are not guided solely by past experience but anticipate the future and look for new solutions. School goals are tied to current research on proven strategies and practices. Research and reflective thought guide actions.

Leadership in Quadrant D (Adaptive Leadership) is the combination of high levels of both application and knowledge. At the highest levels of Quadrant D, students are taking a significant leadership role in the school as well as responsibility for their own learning. Leadership in Quadrant D allows a school to change and adapt more easily through staff collaboration in which everyone shares the same vision and commitment to preparing students for their future.

Dr. Jones continues his work in school leadership at the Successful Practices Network (SPN) in Rexford, New York. The Successful Practices Network is a not-for-profit organization founded in 2003 by Bill and Bonnie Daggett. SPN is committed to helping educators create a culture of rigor, relevance, and relationships for all students. SPN works with schools, districts, regional education centers, state departments of education, and other partner organizations to share resources, data, research, and technical assistance. You can learn more about SPN at: spnetwork.org/.[3]

The Culture Framework

Building on both the original Rigor/Relevance Framework and the Leadership Framework, the Culture Framework is a new mental model, or map, that can guide a school's journey toward creating a more positive, innovative, and effective school culture. It can provide a context for acquiring, applying, and assessing strategies, skills, tools, and processes to guide the improvement of your school culture.

School leadership is not a position but a disposition for taking action. One role of the individual school leader is to broaden the definition of leadership to include the many staff and students as leaders who share a common vision. Quadrant D leadership is the collaborative responsibility for taking action to reach future-oriented goals while meeting the intellectual, emotional, and physical needs of each student.

Each of the International Center's mental models can offer insight into creating a highly effective culture and a map to measure a school's progress. Using the Rigor/Relevance Framework and the Leadership Framework as a guide, I have designed a similar framework that can be used for reflecting on the unique culture of any school. In each of the four quadrants of the Culture Framework, specific cultural characteristics can be identified, and the framework can be used to measure progress from Quadrant A to Quadrant D.

Like the Rigor/Relevance Framework, the Culture Framework can be divided into four quadrants. But unlike the Rigor/Relevance Framework, both the vertical and horizontal axis are labeled along a *trust* continuum. This important distinction is because, more than any other single factor, it is the level of trust within a school's culture that determines the effectiveness of both collaboration and empowerment! No other element comes close. School leaders everywhere understand and agree. So the question is: Why do so many schools spend so little time thinking about it? Working on it? Planning for it?

The author Stephen Covey has written extensively about trust. Covey says, "Without *trust*, we don't truly collaborate; we merely coordinate or, at best, cooperate. It is *trust* that transforms a group of people into a team." He goes on to say, "Trust is the glue of life. It's the most essential ingredient in effective communication. It's the foundational principle that holds all relationships."

In Patrick Lencioni's book, *The Five Dysfunctions of a Team*, he explains that trust is the foundation of all effective teams. He explains why members of great teams must trust one another on a fundamental, emotional level. Most importantly, he says, they are comfortable being vulnerable with each other about their weaknesses, mistakes, fears, and behaviors.

In the Culture Framework, collaboration is on the vertical axis with trust as the variable. Improving collaboration requires raising the ability and effectiveness of any staff to work smarter, not harder, by working collectively to solve problems together. At the lower levels of the collaboration axis, lower levels of trust inhibit every aspect of collaboration, from communication to content. This lack of trust reveals itself often when students, teachers, or administrators are unable or unwilling to be *vulnerable* within their group. As a result, they are less likely to admit their mistakes, communicate openly, share ideas freely, or hold each other accountable for the group's outcomes.

CULTURE FRAMEWORK

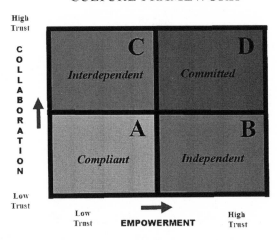

Empowerment is on the horizontal continuum of the Culture Framework, with trust once again as the variable. Empowerment and trust often work in tandem. Lack of trust is the most common reason for lack of authentic empowerment, and lack of empowerment leads to lower trust. Mastering meaningful empowerment is the single most important action school leaders can take to create greater trust . . . and the most powerful strategy teachers can use with students in their classrooms. You see, trust only improves when we practice it.

That means if you want to believe you can trust your students, you must start by trusting your students. Students (and adults) can only become more trustworthy with practice. This can be scary for some, but the result is powerful. When trust is high, empowered teams of students, teachers, or administrators are all more willing and able to take risks, make mistakes, and innovate. We will explore a specific leadership strategy for this in chapter 7, "Release Control," and a powerful set of teacher strategies in chapter 15,

"Classroom Collaboration." But as you will soon see, all the strategies in part II work well at both levels.

A lack of trust at the lower levels of the empowerment continuum means that teachers are often making decisions and solving day-to-day problems on their own. At higher levels, innovative ideas and practices of single teachers or teams are more widely distributed throughout the school culture. Authentic empowerment increases the distribution and density of leadership from a single leader, teacher, or student to an entire school community. It is the single most effective strategy for "growing more leaders" and for creating a culture with a disposition for taking action or, as they say at Farrington, making shift happen!

The Four Quadrants of the Culture Framework

Quadrant A—Compliant

Quadrant A culture is characterized by schools with low levels of trust. When trust is at the lowest levels, both collaboration and empowerment are either not present or not very effective. Too often it describes a traditional school culture where staff works hard but a "check the box" mentality is common. Almost everyone—administrators, instructional leaders, and teachers—focus on doing only what is required; teachers acquire the skills they need and often make decisions independently.

Quad A schools sometimes exhibit all five of the characteristics of a dysfunctional team identified by Patrick Lencioni: *absence of trust* (lack of vulnerability); *fear of conflict* (seek artificial harmony over constructive debate); *lack of commitment* (a "check the box" mentality); *avoidance of accountability* (do not call peers on counterproductive behavior or poor performance); and *inattention to results* (focused on individual success, status, and ego before team success).

But it's important to remember that there are great teachers everywhere. Even in some of the most compliant cultures you will find examples of great teaching and learning, what I call random "pockets of excellence," often in spite of their school's dysfunctional culture. The human spirit is a beautiful thing.

Quadrant B—Independent

A Quad B culture is characterized by schools with higher levels of empowerment, but lower levels of collaboration. In these schools, instructional leaders have managed to build greater trust with their teachers, most often by releasing control. As a result, the teachers have more freedom to experiment and try to do things their own way. While these teachers do feel trusted and empowered to try new methods, their practice is often not guided by a common set of school goals, clearly defined expectations, or even a shared vision. As a result, their instructional delivery does not benefit from being informed, and improved by, collaboration with others. More often, these innovative teachers work in a highly individualized and isolated environment, taking actions which may, or may not, be consistent with the school's vision or goals.

Quadrant C—Interdependent
A Quad C culture is one where trust is high enough between teachers that they have learned to effectively collaborate. But trust is not high enough on the empowerment axis, between teachers and school leaders, that instructional leadership is broadly distributed within the school. As a result, teachers are not yet able to fully translate their collaboration into shared leadership and goal-setting around instructional practice. In a Quad C culture, too many important decisions that impact instruction often remain top-down, even as more effective collaboration offers the potential for both greater teacher buy-in to the school's goals and better problem-solving to reach those goals. These schools have learned how to work smarter, not harder—but not wiser.

Quadrant D—Committed
A Quad D culture is characterized by evidence of high levels of trust, collaboration, and empowerment by all staff, leaders, teachers, and students. These schools are unlikely to show any of Lencioni's five dysfunctions of a team. There is clear evidence that, at the highest levels of Quad D culture, both staff and students are in the habit of holding each other accountable for their own teaching and learning.

Innovation thrives in Quad D schools because their culture allows the school to change and adapt more easily through highly effective staff collaboration, which is broadly shared by a widely distributed leadership process. They are schools in which everyone shares a common vision and commitment to preparing students for the future. They are not guided solely by past experiences. In short, Quad D cultures have learned to work smarter, not harder and distribute the leadership of that work broadly.

Strategies for Creating Quadrant D Culture

As cultures evolve, they often go through all four quadrants of the Culture Framework. But unlike the Rigor/Relevance and Leadership Frameworks, where all quadrants are useful and have their place, the most desirable and effective quadrant of the Culture Framework is Quadrant D. Creating a Quad

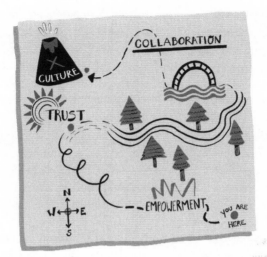

D culture should be the aspiration for all school leaders. However, culture is also in a constant state of change, so there is always a need for leaders to understand the impact of their decisions and actions in all four of the quadrants.

Without well-established relationships and a strategic culture focus, schools often will naturally operate in Quadrant A. Using the Culture Framework as a guide, the goal is to move more toward Quadrant D. That means intentionally (strategically) planning for a more trusting, collaborative, and empowered culture. The better a staff can understand and apply this framework, the more it will help them to better understand their role in distributed leadership and help them become more engaged in decision making.

Increasing Staff and Student Leadership

Moving from Quadrants A and C to Quadrants B and D can be characterized by increasing both staff and student ownership of learning through increased empowerment. At the highest levels of the culture, teachers and students take significant responsibility for their actions. Practices related to distributing school leadership are consistent with moving organizational leadership to Quadrants B and D. Creating various school-based teams to lead school improvement efforts or focus on enhancing school culture or analyzing student data is a good method of increasing staff leadership.

Moving from Quadrants A and B to Quadrants C and D can be characterized by the shift in thinking that guides leadership action and reflecting on the need for increased collaboration within the entire school culture, collaboration that is not simply guided by past practices and traditions. Decisions and actions are based on collaboration and should include paying attention to the future education needs of students to succeed in a complex, rapidly changing world. When school cultures are often found defending the status quo, the culture is at level A. When the school culture passionately pursues higher expectations for all students, is not satisfied with current student achievement, and implements creative solutions, it is more likely functioning at Quadrants C and D.

Culture in Different Quadrants—Determined by Trust Level

Each culture quadrant can be recognized by certain characteristics in a school. Quad A cultures, for example, are often outwardly deceptively calm and friendly. Both staff and students are polite and well-mannered. But a closer look reveals they are simply following the rules and "checking the boxes." They often do their work in isolation with little collaboration or empowerment. They seldom seek, or offer, to help others. A "not my job" attitude is common. The prime directive is: this is the way we've always done it. The rules are set by a traditional chain of command, and the leader is the primary decision maker in the school. Another way to describe these schools is "rule driven." These schools often have little capacity to respond to new challenges, like demographic diversity or new technologies.

While still dependent on a more traditional chain of command to establish the vision and goals, Quad C cultures will often turn to their highly collaborative teams to meet the challenges facing their schools. They may introduce innovations, primarily through the effectiveness of their collaboration, because they are able to "work smarter, not harder." These successful teams will produce isolated pockets of innovation but only a portion of the staff will buy into these ideas. In Quad C cultures, success is not always owned and/ or shared broadly. The success is not systemic largely because the leadership is not distributed, which results in lack of individual ownership and buy-in.

A Quad B culture is characterized by creative and highly empowered individuals each "doing their own thing," often in isolation from the school community as a whole. Indeed, the lack of real community is often what best characterizes Quad B cultures. This could be described as an environment where each member is following their own compass, internally focused and not connecting well with others in the school or community.

A Quad D culture can best be identified by high levels of trust, often measured by their continuous feedback loops and frequent surveys. Their trust is established, strengthened, and maintained through a highly empowered and collaborative way of work. Quad D schools are marked by innovative methods. They are on a clear path to sustained improvement because they involve all staff and students actively in taking responsibility for their own learning.

The leadership in a Quad D school does not reside in a single individual or group but is widely distributed. Teachers and students act every day in ways that support the school's mission. They feel as though they share responsibility for all phases of the school operation and have a strong, trusting relationship with school leaders. Because, together, they made the move from compliant to committed.

Finally, Farrington High School is at the center of this book for a reason. Farrington is an excellent example of a Quad D school where empowered collaboration is so pervasive, it has become their normal way of work. It is a school where highly empowered teachers are given the freedom to explore *Bold School* technology models like blended learning in order to find the implementation that works best for their students and classroom.

In chapter 13, you will learn about Sean Witwer, a SPED math teacher who has gone beyond Quad D lessons to create what can best be described as a Quad D classroom. At Farrington, you will find teachers working within their schoolwide CTE-Academy structure to not only regularly create highly rigorous and relevant, interdisciplinary Quad D lessons but sometimes collaborate across academies as well.

Ultimately, a school with a Quad D culture is a fun place to be! It's a school where the joy of learning is the order of the day, a school where both teachers and students come each day filled with the excitement and passion of discovery. Farrington is a school of teaching and learning, of A'o, for all.

Notes

1. See appendix C.
2. See appendix D.
3. See appendix E.

Brain-Based Strategies to Build a Culture of Learning

You will find more than ten strategies in part II. Each one is a tested and proven strategy shared by the teachers and principals who use them at Farrington and its feeder schools, Kalakaua Middle School and Kalihi Elementary School. Each chapter contains an interview with the person who contributed the strategy. The interview allows for you to meet each of these educators and hear from them directly, in their own voice, about where the strategy came from and how it has changed their classroom or school.

It's important to remember that, whether the strategy comes from a teacher or principal, the big idea behind every strategy will work at both the classroom and school level. For example, building trust is absolutely essential for everyone at every level, and we never do finish. Trust is the foundation of a highly effective classroom or school. And trust is always under construction. Releasing control is essential for building trust and just as important for every teacher. But as we will see in chapter 7, it may be even harder for a strong principal. When it comes to culture, there is no difference between students and adults. The brain chemistry is absolutely the same.

Every strategy in part II is built on a foundation of the same three things: trust, empowerment, and collaboration. These three elements are combined in chapter 5 to form the Culture Framework. The Culture Framework is a mental model, or map, that you can use to reflect on the culture of your classroom or school, where you are now and where you want to go. As you examine each strategy, think about how these three essential elements of trust, empowerment, and collaboration combine.

There are several strategies in part II designed specifically for Special Education and English Language Learner students. They work for *all* students. At the International Center, we have learned that, in a school where SPED and ELL students thrive, *all* students thrive. When you can watch a group of SPED or ELL students guide and reflect on their own Socratic seminar, you will know that rigor is not just possible for some, but for *all*.

Finally, each chapter in part II ends with a strategy template that will walk you through each step of how to apply the strategy in your own classroom or school. Each strategy template contains a link to the brain research behind the specific culture characteristics outlined in chapter 3. Additional supporting materials for each strategy are available in the appendixes.

Trust in Trust

ICLE has been coaching, training, and studying Model Schools for twenty-six years. There is one word to quickly and accurately describe how a Model School is different from other schools: trust. Trust is a must! All highly effective cultures (and relationships) are built on trust. It is the common denominator ICLE has seen across all highly effective schools. It is essential. There simply is no substitute for trust.

As a result, we've been asking educators for years about the level of trust in their schools and districts. We've been surveying, interviewing, and collecting data from hundreds of schools. Overwhelmingly, schools say lack of trust is a problem. So, if trust is so important, why aren't more schools and districts better at creating it? As we learned in chapter 3, no characteristic of culture is more important than trust. And yet . . . no characteristic is as *rare* as trust. Why?

Schools That Trust

ICLE's coaching work has taken them into hundreds of schools and thousands of classrooms across the country. They've learned that every school has its own unique DNA and culture profile. The same is true of every classroom within the school. A school's data will paint a picture of one part of its profile. Staff and student interviews can add qualitative details. But there's no substitute for spending time in classrooms. Given time, a pretty clear profile picture emerges. We've seen culture that ranges from tremendous to toxic.

There's a famous quote by Leo Tolstoy about families from *Anna Karenina*: "Happy families are all alike; every unhappy family is unhappy in its own way." Tolstoy is telling us that happy families all share several essential characteristics. In some ways, the same is true of successful schools. Successful schools share a few common characteristics. Most importantly, they are all schools that trust. They are also generally happy, energetic, and engaging schools. They are filled with people who want to be there. And the same is true of classrooms. Schools that trust share a common vision. Their vision is so compelling, staff can easily repeat it. That's because their vision is what gets them up in the morning, eager and excited about being part of the journey.

In short, these schools know *why* they are going *where* they are going and *what* they're doing to get there. They went slow at first, to build a strong consensus around each of these three things. As a result, they don't waste time dividing into "us" against "them."

The staff in these schools have learned to trust one another on a deep, emotional level. They are comfortable being vulnerable about their mistakes, weaknesses, and fears. They can be completely open with each other without a need to "watch what they say."

Schools that trust speak a common language. They have clear team norms, protocols, and processes. And most importantly, they are willing to take risks without a guarantee of success.

Schools That Don't Trust

The staff in schools that don't trust do not trust each other. They do not share a common vision. They do not like to collaborate on projects and sometimes even look for ways to avoid spending time together. They do not share information openly but rather hoard it as currency—or even a weapon to use against others. They tend to conceal their mistakes and weaknesses. And they hesitate to ask for help or feedback on a problem.

Like neurotic individuals, cultures that grow toxic can become not just ineffective but dysfunctional. Seldom do members volunteer to help outside their specific area of responsibility. They waste a good deal of time managing their behaviors. They are quick to jump to negative conclusions and often hold grudges.

While working with teachers in one elementary school to use more collaborative instructional strategies with their students, an ICLE coach planned to use grade-level teams to model the approach. But the principal, who was new to the building, told the coach he might as well forget about fifth grade. "Collaborate?" she said. "They don't talk to each other. They don't even *like* each other." Sure enough, that group had a hard time being in the same room. How very sad for them and their students.

But it wasn't just fifth grade. The culture of the whole school was truly toxic. Dysfunction and dishonesty were everywhere. To be fair, they'd had four principals in five years, and this new one was not so sure she wanted to stay. But at least the principal recognized that if your culture is broken you can't fix anything else. So our instructional coach started on building culture. But the school had been such a problem that the principal was worried the district wouldn't give her the time she'd need.

Yes, building trust takes time. But you can't just wait for trust to happen. In chapter 3 we learned about the chemistry of culture discoveries emerging from Paul Zak's lab regarding specific behaviors shown to release oxytocin in our brain and the direct relationship between oxytocin and trust. These discoveries indicate that the most important ingredient in building trust is not time—it is behavior and courage, specifically the courage to be vulnerable. In other words, no amount of time will produce trust in a toxic culture. The culture will not change until the behaviors change.

Building trust requires the courage to be vulnerable with others, particularly when we don't know whether our vulnerability will be respected or returned. But it is only when we are comfortable being honest, honestly exposed, vulnerable, unafraid to admit our mistakes, willing to be wrong, and ask for help that true trust develops.

Contrary to what most people believe, trust is not some soft, illusive quality that you either have or you don't; rather, trust is a pragmatic, tangible, actionable asset that you can create—much faster than you probably think possible.

—Steven Covey

Ultimately, trust is all about *vulnerability*. Schools who trust are comfortable being open to one another, open and honest about their weaknesses, failures, and fears. To build trust, you and your staff must be willing to take risks without a guarantee of success. In schools that trust, both administrators and teachers are able to be vulnerable with each other and with their students. If you want to increase the trust of your staff, you must begin by being vulnerable. You must model the behaviors you want to see.

In the troubled elementary school above, the principal decided she had to start at the very beginning and lay a new foundation. The coach led staff workshops on the most common dysfunctions of a team (some of the staff recognized they had them all). We did team-building exercises. We led workshops on relationship-building. And the principal was willing to model being vulnerable. Slowly, using school climate surveys, the culture of the school began to improve and grow more positive.

Inside schools that trust you will find a pervasive Growth Mindset (more about this later). Schools that trust are not afraid to make mistakes because they have come to see mistakes not as failures but as gateways to learning. Their Growth Mindset extends from the principal's office to each classroom and touches everyone.

One powerful way leaders build trust is by establishing a common, compelling vision, creating clear expectations, providing staff what they need, and getting out of their way.[1] Building trust in the classroom or school is not about expecting less from students or staff. Just the opposite: high-trust schools hold everyone accountable but without micromanaging them. Students and teachers learn to trust because they are trusted.

Over the years, few schools have been more effective at building a positive culture for its students and staff than Farrington High School. As we saw in chapter 2, it is the "Farrington Way" that best brings the story to life. And there may be no better way to understand creating culture than by using Farrington and its principal, Al Carganilla, as a guide. Farrington's journey from struggling to successful provides an excellent description of one highly effective implementation of the process. This book is deeply indebted to Farrington instructional leaders and teachers for generously sharing their story in this book.

You were introduced to the Farrington principal, Al Carganilla, in chapter 4. In some ways Al was uniquely positioned to guide Farrington's journey. He was born to two immigrant parents from the Philippines and grew up in Honolulu's lower Kalihi neighborhood, not a mile from Farrington, where he went to school and where he still lives. One of the first things you quickly notice about Al is his total commitment to the school and his community.

Al is also a talented and successful coach. So from the beginning he understood and supported ICLE's leadership and instructional coaching role. As the Farrington leadership team began to identify goals and objectives, Al immediately identified relationships and culture as a priority. He clearly understood that of ICLE's 3 Rs—rigor, relevance, and relationships—the third R, relationships, had to come first. In fact, he had been working on Farrington's culture since he arrived and was making measurable progress.

But from the first coaching sessions, Al made it clear that while much of the Farrington staff were on board, he was not satisfied with the level of "buy-in" from the rest. He believed too many were compliant rather than committed. The annual State of Hawaii School Quality Survey (SQS) data confirmed that trust was not where it should be, with staff often unwilling to try new things. Because when trust is low, so is innovation.

You're Pre-Forgiven

In one early coaching session, as Al was trying to understand and explain the slow progress of teachers' instructional improvement and willingness to try innovative methods, he said, "Our teachers can try almost anything they think will be good for students. Don't they know they're pre-forgiven?" That struck me as profoundly simple. So I repeated his question and asked him: if he really believed that, why didn't the teachers know it? And if they knew it, why didn't they believe it?

From that early conversation, Al's pre-forgiven strategy was born, as we began to explore how he could begin to build a more positive culture of commitment and innovation. We decided to focus on three things: trust, empowerment, and collaboration. Of these three things, trust is first and most essential element. To build trust we decided to turn Al's pre-forgiven phrase into a mantra, a kind of tag line that would be repeated school wide. But I'd rather let him explain it in his own words.

Interview with Al Carganilla

What does "You're pre-forgiven" mean to you?

The whole mantra of "You are pre-forgiven" came from my first principal, Dennis Manalili, whom I worked for when I was an assistant principal at Kaimuki High School. In 2003, as he mentored me during my first year, he sat me down and told me, "You don't need to come up to me every time you have a problem. You have the answer, but you need to work hard to find it. If you do something wrong, don't worry about it; you are pre-forgiven."

Being a new assistant principal, I felt so empowered by that statement. I felt so supported and was motivated to do my best in every situation. It was only when I took my first principalship in 2006 that I realized the importance of that mantra.

Being a new principal at Hokulani Elementary, I was eager to start my new job and I was full of excitement, but I didn't realize how complex the position was with the myriad responsibilities. Not having an assistant principal on staff due to the low enrollment (240 students) of the elementary school, I was responsible for every aspect of school operations. Classroom teachers, office operations, cafeteria food services, custodians, repair and maintenance, educational assistants, contracted providers, special education, after-school programs, and before-school care are just some of the things I had to control. I was totally overwhelmed, but I kept at it.

I have always been huge on building and sustaining positive relationships, so the first goal was to ensure that I focused on creating a family atmosphere at the school where everyone supported one another. I also need to be transparent and lead from a place of vulnerability. All the stakeholders needed to know who I am and the core values that are important for our organization to succeed.

It was an amazing three years as I learned a lot about myself and leadership. As I was about to introduce my pre-forgiven mantra that I got from my mentor, I interviewed and was offered the job at Farrington High School, the biggest public high school in the state of Hawaii and my alma mater.

Why did you decide to make "You're pre-forgiven" sort of your mantra?

Once at Farrington High School, I had to make that notion of "You are pre-forgiven" my mantra because it was important to have my staff feel what I felt when Principal Manalili sat me down and said that statement to me. Moving from a staff of about thirty-five adults at Hokulani Elementary to more than three hundred adults at Farrington High School, it was a huge transition but a very exciting time.

Being an alumnus of Farrington High School, and having some of my former high school teachers still on staff, building trust and credibility were the first tasks on my agenda. As a college baseball athlete, then a high school baseball and football coach, I was a fierce competitor and control freak. I needed to make sure that I was in control of my teammates, my players, and every situation I was in. I needed to be in charge, and in decisions that didn't go my way, I needed to voice my opinion and my side of how I felt.

Moving to Farrington, I realized that needed to change. There was no way I would be able to do it alone. I needed the help of all my five assistant principals and various leaders on campus. I needed to give up control and begin to support everyone so they could reinforce the vision and mission of our organization. That is when I decided to let everyone know, "You are pre-forgiven." I also informed them to let me know how I can support them along our journey toward excellence. Wow!! I didn't know that small statement would go a long way in empowering our teachers to do the best work they are capable of.

I reflected on how empowered I was as a new assistant principal. I began to hear expressions of gratitude that our teachers felt when they were encouraged to try new things without the fear of failure. There was a renewed sense of energy in our classrooms and on campus. I could see confidence and feel the energy in the teachers and staff. That helped our entire school organization to build positive and meaningful relationships that would allow us to grow and collaborate at a high level. Without the trust, there is no way that the critical conversations that are needed to improve curriculum, pedagogy, and most importantly relationships would take place.

Can you give us an example of how you've used pre-forgiven with a teacher?

I know that the pre-forgiven strategy has worked for all our teachers when it comes to academic freedom and taking the initiative to try new things in the classroom as evidenced by the great things happening in our classrooms: the video project in Sean Witwer's class, the interdepartment and interacademy projects that have taken place like the food truck project and the PE project with Kalihi Elementary. It's just awesome to know that the teachers feel supported that they could try anything regardless if they fail or not. The goal of the pre-forgiven strategy extends beyond the teachers feeling bold and creative to try new things. I want them to at some point extend that to pre-forgive their students to try new things as well and incorporate the student voice we all want in our schools. For instance, if the teacher assigns a project, I want the students to do the projects in different ways: PowerPoint presentation, build a model, create a rap or song, etc. That would be incredible if we can do that at a schoolwide level. If a student fails, pre-forgive them and give them another shot at doing it in another way to see if they definitely grasped the concept.

Have you ever had a teacher take advantage of your pre-forgiven policy?

I can't think of a time when a teacher blatantly took advantage of the pre-forgiven strategy. I know a couple times a few teachers purchased items and wanted to get reimbursed but they didn't know the process so couldn't get reimbursed. I actually did forgive them and signed letters to send to procurement to see if I could reimburse them. I then shared the process with them and the entire staff so they knew how to get reimbursed. I know a few times teachers came in late and said, "Am I pre-forgiven?" I said yes, but if it's chronic, then you won't be pre-forgiven because it's your responsibility to get here on time. For the most part there really isn't a time where they have taken advantage of it. They know that that strategy is really for the classroom and trying new things. They don't need to do the same things in biology or math classes. They can have the same outcomes but do different things in getting there. The strategy has really helped our teachers explore great ways of doing things.

In what ways do you think it has made a difference for Farrington?

The biggest impact the "You are pre-forgiven" statement made was empowering our teachers and staff to problem solve and make decisions that they felt were right. They weren't afraid to make mistakes. A lot of school staffs around the country go through their work day as if they are walking on egg shells and afraid of making a mistake because of the fear of what might come from administration.

There has always been an us vs. you attitude when it comes to teachers and administration. That's how it was at Farrington. There just wasn't that trust with administration so something needed to be done. That mantra of "You are pre-forgiven" was a game changer. It allowed the staff to build trust with administration and finally believe that we were in their corner and truly supported them.

More importantly, it allowed everyone to do what they were trained to do. The teachers began to be more innovative and thinking out of the box to meet their students' needs. It gave teachers discretion on how to do their work. Departments and academies had end goals but how you get there was left to each individual teacher. They started to take ownership of their profession and slowly began to hold everyone accountable. Critical conversations increased. Discussions were all about kids, and attitudes changed from selfishness to selflessness. The whole athletic mantra and feeling at Farrington of "One team, One family" began to spread on campus.

Teacher attitudes and behaviors started to change. The belief that "All students can learn at high levels" increased from 74 percent in 2011 to 86 percent in 2016. The belief that "Student learning depends on positive relationships" and "Teacher collaboration leads to increased student achievement" shot up to 93 percent and 91 percent respectively. Teacher satisfaction also increased from 51.8 percent to 72.5 percent. Great things are happening at Farrington because we are moving from the us vs. you attitude to one of teamwork and family.

How has it changed the culture for the students in your classrooms?

We are certainly not where we want to be with the test and achievement scores, but we are seeing the changes in our classrooms in terms of positive behavior and engagement. Increased teacher positive behavior has allowed our students to trust our teachers as well. Our teachers have increased the expectations in their classrooms, but by being more nurturing and encouraging, their students are putting more effort in the classroom.

We also have focused on moving from "average to excellent" and encouraging our students to "Be the Difference" in their community. The collaborations between different departments and academies have allowed our students to be engaged at a higher level. They too are taking ownership of their own learning as evidenced by peers helping one another as well as the higher level of questioning of one another in their respective classrooms. Socratic seminar activities in classrooms are rich in content and individual voice.

As teachers begin to implement different engagement strategies, students are gaining more confidence in their individual abilities and are not afraid to express their own opinions. Students support one another more and are given many opportunities to collaborate with one another in class. They are moving from passive to active learners and learning new academic and life skills. Students too are being innovative in their classrooms and being more accountable for their work. A different learning culture is taking place and we definitely see growth and we are confident that it will translate to higher test scores in the near future.

What advice would you give other principals who are trying to build trust with their staff?

The biggest advice I would give other principals is to "self-reflect, self-assess, and self-adjust."[2] Take a look at your school and culture and see what changes you are willing to make. Are you clearly communicating expectations? Are you modeling behaviors you want to see in your staff? Are you transparent in everything you do? Are you ready to give up control? For schools to improve and change, administration needs to change.

I certainly made a change in my leadership style. I did a lot of reflection, and in the end, I put the big old chip on my shoulder and my huge ego in my back pocket because I needed to listen to my teachers as their voices were very important. They go through the daily grind in the classrooms every day and they make the biggest impact on student achievement.

In the May 2017 EL Educational Leadership article by Jane Modoono titled "The Trust Factor," she said that building a school culture of trust is an intentional act that benefits principals, teachers, and students. She also said, "After more than 30 years as a school leader, I have come to believe that trust is the most important factor in building a collaborative and positive school culture."

Trusting teachers communicates that you value them and believe in them. Teachers who are trusted take risks and collaborate with their colleagues. They work longer hours. They are committed to maintaining a healthy

Table 6.1. Strategies for Building a Positive Culture

Strategy: *You Are Pre-Forgiven*
Al Carganilla, Principal

This strategy links to the following brain-based research from the chemistry of culture characteristics in chapter 3:

1. Show vulnerability.
2. Release control.
3. Create "challenge stress."
4. Recognize excellence.
5. Share information broadly.
6. Intentionally build relationships.

Brain research shows that trust is essential for building a positive school culture. Trust is the foundation upon which everything else rests. One way we can increase trust is by creating a culture that does not penalize failure. Instead, look for concrete ways to encourage others to innovate by taking risks.

Studies show people are often afraid to try new things because they're afraid to fail. Principal Al Carganilla's mantra, "You're pre-forgiven," is a simple but powerful strategy that communicates clearly to all staff that they are free to innovate without fear of failure. This strategy links directly to all six leadership characteristics identified in Paul Zak's neuroscience research.

Multiple neuroscientific studies show there are few things we can do to more effectively build a positive culture than build trust. To do that we should think and plan as strategically for building trust as we do for our budget.

Step 1	**Reflect on why showing staff and students that you trust them is so important for your classroom, school, or district.**
	1. As a leader, what are your personal strengths?
	2. What specific actions do you take that demonstrate trust?
	3. What are your challenges?
	4. What specific actions can you take?
Step 2	**Plan three actions you can take to demonstrate trust.**
	1. What will you do in each plan?
	2. When will you do them?
	3. How will you communicate each action to your staff?
	4. How are they related and how do they each build trust?
	5. What do you need to prepare?
	6. How will you measure the results?
Step 3	**Deliver your three actions.**
Step 4	**Review your three actions.**
	Begin by reviewing each of the six steps in each plan. What went well? What will you do differently?
Step 5	**Revise your three plans and/or create a new one.**
	After reviewing each of the six steps in your three plans:
	1. Will you continue? Why or why not?
	2. What changes will you make going forward?
	3. What will you do differently next time?

culture—a place where everyone looks forward to coming to work. Most important, they build on this foundation of trust and collaboration to create engaging, rigorous learning opportunities for their students.

Notes

1. See appendix F.
2. See appendix G.

Chapter 7

Release Control

After some sincere self-reflection, a principal currently being coached by ICLE admitted that, yes, she was a "total control freak." For Lorelei Aiwohi, principal of Kalakaua Middle School in the heart of Honolulu's Kalihi neighborhood, this was a leadership breakthrough. While she had achieved many of her goals at Kalakaua Middle School and was seeing improved student outcomes, she knew that if her school was going to take it to the next level, she was going to need better staff buy-in and commitment. She began by assessing her own leadership style and how that was connected to her childhood.

Principal Aiwohi shared that she recognized she was a textbook Quad A—command and control, my way or the highway—leader. But the truth is she'd already taken the hardest and most essential step by owning it. Honest self-reflection is often the most difficult part. (How many teachers would benefit from the same self-awareness?) Then she made a simple plan. She decided that the first question she would have her leadership coach ask on each visit was: how have you released control this month?

Lorelei came to understand that releasing control does not mean giving up accountability, just thinking about accountability in a new way. To successfully release control to others, school leaders need to learn how to facilitate the creation of high but attainable goals, define exactly what success looks like with clear expectations . . . then get out of the way!

Isn't this exactly what we also want to see teachers do more often in their classrooms—release control and transfer the ownership of the learning to the students? Can we really expect to see our teachers facilitate more collaborative student learning in their classrooms if school leaders don't first support and model the process?

This conversation about control is becoming more common among both principals and teachers. Some of these principals and teachers are recognized as our best. They care about kids and they are passionate about learning. While many do recognize they have a control problem, they struggle to let go. Why should this be so hard?

The answer often goes back to the power of our mental models that we talked about in chapter 5. Many of these teachers had been trained in "traditional" stand-and-deliver instruction. That's how they were taught and how they were taught to teach. But they now find themselves facing not only the changing demands of new standards and assessments but students who are most definitely wired differently. As a result, they are beginning to understand the need for more collaboration and student voice using the academic language of their content. But the students can't talk if the teacher never stops!

Many of our best "traditional" teachers are still prisoners of a "traditional" mental model of what a good teacher is. A little voice in the back of their head says, "If I didn't *say* it to them, I didn't teach them. I didn't do my job." Many of these teachers are some of our best at leading a class to the one right answer. They are conditioned by the traditional mental model of a "good" teacher to hate wait time! Any student silence or struggle is a sign that they are failing.

We have learned together that for these teachers to release control, the first thing they need is a new mental model of what a good teacher is. That sounds so simple that many teachers and principals just skip right over it. But the brain research we explored in chapter 3 says mental models are powerful . . . and changing them takes time, practice, and patience.

The Rigor/Relevance Framework is a useful first step in this learning process. The goal of Quad D learning is for the student to do the thinking and working. Contrast that with Quad A instruction where the teacher is doing all the work while the student observes.

Make no mistake, the illusion of control can be dangerous. If we count on control to make us feel good, we will constantly be disappointed by those around us—and life. We will seldom be able to sustain satisfaction. The only thing that control can deliver is frequent frustration. And if you're one of those true "control freaks" who try to control every little detail—for example, the exact wording of the faculty meeting agenda—well, let's just say those are often some of the unhappiest and most stressed-out people you will find. Why can't they see how life constantly conspires to thwart them?

The need for control can seriously erode our sense of well-being and damage our relationships with others. It establishes a fear-based pattern based on our need for stability and predictability in our relationship with others and the world around us. Sadly, our desire to take charge often only creates an illusion of control. This trait can often be observed in school leaders and teachers, many of whom decided to go into education precisely because they wanted to be in control.

Unfortunately, the more we try to micromanage our staff or students, the more likely we are to be dissatisfied with their performance, and we make it less likely that they are able to take ownership of their own learning. But if we can learn to let go of the need to control, we can create conditions that empower more creativity and collaboration in others.

Let's be clear about this: highly effective Quad D student learning *requires* the teacher to release control. Period. It's actually essential, not just nice to have. The same is true for school leaders trying to create a Quad D culture, a culture of learning.

Releasing control requires all of us, teachers and principals, to develop not just a greater tolerance for mistakes but to actually encourage them (more on this later). Rather than reacting negatively or taking harsh corrective action, by using a Growth Mindset, a Quad D culture treats mistakes as opportunities to facilitate learning. Creating a learning culture has been a focus of the work at Farrington High School, and Principal Aiwohi is committed to doing the same at Kalakaua Middle School.

Interview with Lorelei Aiwohi

You're not alone. I've coached many school leaders, and even more teachers, who will admit they have trouble releasing control. Why do you think it was so hard for you personally?

My mother is Portuguese from a strong Catholic middle-class family who had a dairy farm in the Iao Valley on the island of Maui. My father is Hawaiian, Portuguese, and sort of Mormon. My grandparents were sort of married less than the years they were separated, and their children were all distributed to various family, boarding schools, etc., as were most of the children born during the years when they were not married.

My parents were very young when I was born, just turned nineteen. I was the only girl, the oldest of four children. My parents' marriage started off rocky and remained that way. By the time they were twenty, they had three children. My dad worked three jobs and my mom worked at the bakery at night and as a phlebotomist during the day.

As the eldest and only girl, I became "bossy" at a very young age. The control issues . . . not always a struggle, more often for survival started early . . . so to release . . . oh my!!! Being in charge comes with great responsibility, and of course, the only way to get it right is to do it yourself. This is what I believed during my early years of being a principal. This is how I operated. These were the NCLB years. Numbers mattered. But I was tired. It worked as I led small elementary schools that functioned well.

As I moved on to become principal at Kalakaua Middle School, there were many students, many employees, many challenges, so many moving parts. I struggled to connect it all. I couldn't do it by myself. I was really tired.

But . . . I didn't know how to *trust*. Therefore, I struggled with building *relationships*. The hardest part was being vulnerable and allowing anyone to get to me. As Principal Aiwohi, I bring my A game to work—200+ percent—but Lorelei the person never shows up. Allowing that to happen was hard. I was principal here for five years before I opened a school year up at our faculty meeting with sharing that I had a family, personal interests, personal goals, and a professional why.

That was the start of the culture change at Kalakaua Middle School. My vulnerability and openness became the example/model needed for others to open up beyond their "cliques" and start to embrace each other as a whole.

Can you describe a breakthrough moment?

One of my breakthroughs happened last school year as we, the leadership team and I, were planning and restructuring our PLTs to fit our focus of building relationships. As we were planning, I asked how I could support the PLTs. One of the coaches, the bravest one, responded with "You need to stay away." And I was like . . . back to control 101 . . . "What! You think I'm the problem!!" After counting to 10, I mean 110, I realized that was exactly what was needed.

It was obvious that my presence during Professional Learning Time, at meetings, in classrooms, or anywhere brings out a different response to when I am not there. So, with bruised ego and mixed emotions, I agreed to it. This entire first quarter, I have stepped back and let coaches, facilitators, teacher leaders lead. They have done a fabulous job. The trust they have built, the ideas that have generated, and the buy-in from teachers have been remarkable.

Of course, I read all the minutes, do a lot of listening, and still give opinions (when asked) and have very deep conversations with coaches and teacher leaders. I think they appreciate feeling valued and sometimes they even work hard just to impress me. I like the products that teacher leaders come up with, stuff I would never have even dreamed of . . . and so do the teachers. I still feel very much a part of the process and feel like a stronger leader as I am able to lead at a higher level. I still feel very much in control, especially about three weeks ago when one of the coaches shared that the teachers asked if I would attend the PLTs sometimes!!! I am still tired . . . but feel a renewed energy because now I carve time out to spend with students on campus and visit more classrooms.

What would you say to another principal who is struggling to release control?

What I would say to any principal, new or old (us seasoned ones have a harder time), is the same thing that Farrington High School principal Al Carganilla told me: "Be vulnerable; it's okay to let them see who you are."

Table 7.1. Strategies for Building a Positive Culture

Strategy: *Release Control*
Lorelei Aiwohi, Principal

This strategy links to the following brain-based research from the chemistry of culture characteristics in chapter 3:

1. Show vulnerability.
2. Release control.
3. Create "challenge stress."
4. Recognize excellence.
5. Share information broadly.
6. Intentionally build relationships.

Releasing control is such a powerful strategy because it links directly to all six leadership characteristics identified in Paul Zak's neuroscience research.

Multiple scientific studies show there are few things we can do to more effectively build a positive culture. That means we should think as strategically about releasing control as we do for our budget.

Common sense tells us that when teachers and students are given more choices about which projects they'll work on, and/or how they'll represent their work, their engagement and motivation increase.

To successfully release control, we must learn how to create high but attainable goals, define exactly what success looks like with clear expectations . . . and then get out of the way.

Being trusted to figure things out is a big motivator. Surveys show that nearly half of employees would give up a 20 percent raise for greater control over how they work.

Step 1	Reflect on why releasing control is important for you.
	1. What are your strengths?
	2. What are your barriers?
	3. What do you want to change?

Table 7.1. (*continued*)

Step 2	**Plan one way you will release control this week.**
	1. How will you release control?
	2. Where and when will you release control?
	3. Who will be affected?
	4. How will you prepare others to receive the control?
	5. Do you need to prepare materials or resources?
	6. How will you measure the results?
Step 3	**Keep plans in a weekly "control journal."**
	Enter your plans in a weekly journal describing the specific actions you take, or words you say, to release control to others, either students in your class or the staff in your school.
Step 4	**Review the plans in your journal each week.**
	Begin by reviewing each of the six steps in your weekly Journal. What went well? What will you do differently?
Step 5	**Revise your existing plan and create new one.**
	After reviewing each of the six steps in last week's plan:
	1. Will you continue? Why or why not?
	2. What changes will you make going forward?
	3. What will you do differently next time?
	Plan at least one new way to release control next week:
	1. How will you release control?
	2. Where and when will you release control?
	3. Who will be affected?
	4. How will you prepare others to receive the control?
	5. Do you need to prepare materials or resources?
	6. How will you measure the results?

Chapter 8

Empower Others

Cindy Werkmeister is a third-generation Japanese American. Cindy's grand-parents on both sides came to Hawaii from Japan and Okinawa to work on the sugar plantations. But Cindy's grandparents made sure that her parents got an education and graduated from college. Later, Cindy would marry an-other teacher, Scott, who is Japanese, Irish, and German, thus her last name, Werkmeister.

Cindy's father was a banker and her mother a teacher. She credits her mother's influence for her wanting to be a teacher. Cindy said, "The thing I remember is that she was always home with my brothers and I and was a supportive mother and teacher. At first, I wanted to be an interior designer. I changed my mind when I traveled to Europe after my junior year in college. I remember seeing the sights of Europe thinking, how come I didn't learn this in school? That inspired me to pursue teaching social studies in high school."

When Cindy started her current position fifteen years ago as Farrington's strategic planner, Farrington was a Title I, inner-city school in Needs Im-provement status, and their scores were not improving. They had a 5 percent math proficiency and 11 percent reading. They knew that unless they could show improvement, they would fall into restructuring and face the very real threat of school takeover.

Cindy dug into the school improvement research and found several fac-tors consistently contributing to school improvement: developing teacher leadership, teacher collaboration, assessment for learning, and administrative walkthroughs. She decided to focus on the first three, believing that while administrative walkthroughs can help, establishing peer visits is better for the overall culture of the school.

By listening to teachers, Cindy learned that effective teachers wanted administrative walkthroughs to validate their work and as a way to identify teachers who need support. But she didn't think administrators were best-suited to coach them. Too often, the principal-teacher relationship can get in the way of real growth. And she was not convinced administrators have the time for consistent long-term teacher support. Cindy deeply believed that, ultimately, teachers empowering teachers is the best path to creating a more positive, trusting culture where continuous improvement can take place for all teachers.

Cindy's unwavering commitment to creating a unique culture of collaboration at Farrington has been an essential element of their success. Working side by side with Principal Carganilla, she helped to make his vision a reality and together they have transformed the school.

Today, Farrington is a three-time National Model School and has twice presented the story of their remarkable journey to thousands of educators at the National Model Schools Conference. ICLE leadership and instructional coaches have recognized that one of the most important factors in their success has been their consistent focus, the ability to keep their eye on the ball, and to keep the main thing the main thing. Unlike so many schools who jump from program to program, they have maintained a laser-like focus on doing three things well: trust, empowerment, and collaboration.

Cindy's fifteen-year history with the Farrington High School culture gives her a unique perspective on their journey from a struggling to a successful school. Her commitment and experience has been invaluable to the Farrington staff, so we asked if she would like to close her own circle by sharing some of the highlights from her unique perspective.

Interview with Cindy Werkmeister

You've been at Farrington longer than anyone on the leadership team. Can you tell us a little more about the history of Farrington's unique culture of collaboration and empowerment?

A teacher empowering teacher's culture does not happen overnight; for our school I would say it took maybe ten years? Depending on the culture of your school, it might be more or less. It requires a vision of what you want your culture to look like, the right people, patience, and a safe environment based on trust and collaboration. Ten years ago, my principal at the time had a vision based on Professional Learning Communities, a vision that I also believed would move our school in a positive direction.

The problem was we didn't have key people to help move a faculty as big as ours and our teachers did not trust each other enough. We were still teaching in solos and collaboration was not the norm. I was doing most of the professional development for 160 faculty for our school by myself. I realized we had a culture problem.

Changing this culture was going to be difficult. We needed to start slowly with non-threatening resources. We began by reading articles on topics that reinforced the importance of teacher collaboration, how assessment for learning can improve student performance, and what are the important skills students need to succeed in the twenty-first century, but it can be anything your school is focusing on. The purpose is to break down the silos.

I work in lots of schools that are trying to create more collaboration, to break down the silos, as you call them. How exactly did Farrington go about doing that?

Once teachers began to feel comfortable discussing articles, we started to discuss student work. Early on, we knew we wouldn't get anyone to share their student work. We were not ready for that. I collected student work from trainings that I had been to and from Internet sites. Some sites had grading rubrics as well. Teachers could be open and honest with anonymous work. That way they could share their ideas for improvement using other teachers' work and hopefully apply it to their own classrooms or lessons without feeling judged.

Eventually we decided to train all teachers, even the PE and CTE teachers, in how to design constructive response questions and what to look for in student work. Next everyone had to create one and assign it and collect student work to look at. Then at a faculty meeting, teachers brought in samples of student work in assigned groups of three to four. The results were mixed.

Some groups were able to honestly talk about the work; others had teachers who didn't bring work or brought work from another teacher's class. Discussion was deep in some and limited in others. Although discussion protocols were in place, teachers were not used to using protocols and did not follow them.

For a first attempt, it was a learning experience. I think the teachers who took it seriously got a lot out of it, but if we were going to change culture, we needed an overwhelming majority to do it with fidelity and move from compliance to buy-in. In hindsight, we should have spent more time on ice breakers and team building before discussing the work.

One thing in our favor at the time is that we did see a big jump in our reading scores, which was good for making the argument for having a school-wide focus; even though the scores were not high, it was enough to keep us out of restructuring.

What else was happening at that time?

In addition, that year we had to deal with a WASC recommendation to align our curriculum and develop common assessments. Department chair roles were changing too because we knew that if we were going to make any progress in these areas, the department chairs needed to play a bigger role. They had to do more than just administrative stuff; they had to be responsible for monitoring the curriculum, instruction, and assessment.

This was an important shift that not every department chair was ready for. But with time, encouragement, and support, they have embraced the role. It was rough in the beginning. We tried to let course-alike teams work without close supervision. However, we soon realized that teams were not really meeting and collaborating in a meaningful way. Again, it was more out of just compliance.

So we regrouped and had all members of several departments meet in one place so that a few of the teacher leaders could provide support to teams in one location. What we observed was a lot of pushback. We assumed it would take a semester of meeting once a week for an hour after school to get the curriculum maps done.

Mind you, we were not asking for pacing guides. We just wanted teachers to agree on essential units, what standards would be addressed in those units, essential content and skills to be taught. We did not require unit or lesson plans, and teachers could teach these units any way they wanted. The goal was to create a common final based on standards identified so that teachers could reflect on the results and share what they thought went well so others could do those successful strategies in their classrooms.

We wanted the best instruction to be shared so all students would have great instruction.

It took one semester for anyone to put pen to paper. There was a lot of mistrust and a feeling that this was the flavor of the month and this too shall pass. We continued to meet and reassured teachers that no one was going to evaluate their work and units can always be revised and that the goal was to learn from each other.

We persisted and stayed the course. It really wasn't until about two years later that teachers began to move from compliance to beginning to believe in the process. Today, four years later, teachers are asking for sub days to collaborate on lessons and are posting their lessons online for all to share.

What happened next?

Several things happened at this point. We got a new principal, Al Carganilla, who was deeply committed to teacher collaboration and empowerment. We were up for a full WASC visit, and we were directed by our complex area superintendent to hire a consultant to help us improve instruction and test scores. We decided to hire a consultant to help us develop learning teams.

At the time, this seemed to be a natural next step. The process was in line with collaboration, designing effective lessons, assessment for learning, and revising lessons after reflecting on the results. We didn't have enough leaders to help monitor the results, so we didn't do this schoolwide. Freshmen and sophomore English, social studies, Algebra I, and science teams were the first to learn the process. The teams were made up of teachers who had worked together over a few years. The teams that did better were teams with leaders who had the ability to work well with people and knew curriculum.

At that time, teachers were still used to planning lessons in silos and certainly were not used to collaborating on a common lesson. Getting agreement took time. Looking back, we should have done more work on developing leadership, facilitation, and teaming skills such as developing norms for working together. In addition, teams still needed to be monitored closely.

Trusting that teachers would "get it" and buy in would have been a mistake at this point. Although some teachers were doing it for compliance, others did want to try it but wanted to do it right and were afraid of making mistakes. Being "pre-forgiven" for honest mistakes was not ingrained in our culture yet.

And how did Principal Carganilla react?

Through all of this, Principal Carganilla's vision of a school based on a collaborative culture rich in best practices has never wavered. As a succession of consultants came in, each had to align to that goal. Naturally, when ICLE came in, there was some skepticism. What ICLE brought to the table was a common vision for what rigorous, relevant, and engaging lessons should look like. From the start, the ultimate goal was to plan lessons with Quad D in mind. The Rigor/Relevance rubric was the target for teachers to plan their lessons around, and we asked teachers to create a common Quad D lesson plan template.

With all these pieces in place, we felt we were ready. We decided to kick off the 2015–2016 school year in a special way. To communicate the importance of our next steps, we held a two-day workshop in a beautiful off-campus conference center and treated teachers to a delicious lunch. Jim Warford opened that day, laying out a compelling case for our new 3Rs: relationships, relevance, and rigor.

Everyone was given an overview of what that meant in smaller breakouts. Although everyone got the overview, we really focused the hard work on academy teachers. They were not happy being pulled out for monthly full-day PD. There was some pushback in the beginning, but as teachers began planning together, they saw that having dedicated time during the school day to plan made their lives a bit easier because although they had to make lesson plans, they had time to create some amazing lessons that they could use in their academies.

One group of teachers took it a step further and created not only interdisciplinary but interacademy rigorous, engaging, real-world units. Students from the Business Academy taught Culinary Academy students how to develop a marketing plan for their food trucks. English and math teachers also contributed. Although students didn't build actual food trucks, they did have to pitch their business plans, complete with sample food items and menus, to a panel of industry judges in a *Shark Tank*–type activity.

The Engineering Academy collaborated on a catapult project that involved physics, math, social studies, English, and building construction classes. The success of these projects, along with the high levels of student engagement and excitement teachers saw, made buy-in for year two much easier. There was still some grumbling but not like year one. More teachers collaborated with minimal pushback. At the end of the second year, we had teachers create posters explaining their Quad D lessons with student work. It was on display for all teachers to see.

How do you think that set the stage for the next year?

During the 2017–2018 school year, teachers really stepped up their game. The Engineering Academy partnered with the World Surf League (WSL) and are designing and building models of a merchandise trailer for WSL. Students have to pitch their drawings and models to the WSL, who will select one to build.

The next year, the Building and Construction class will work with WSL to build the trailer. The Farrington Creative Arts and Technology Academy English, Graphics Arts, and Arts and Communication Core teachers collaborated on a vectoring project that started the drawing in the Core class, moved to students creating vector characters from the drawing, and English students writing the character analysis of each character.

Today, we have so many requests from teachers who want to take a sub day to work on Quad D lessons and we don't monitor any of them. We trust that they will use the time wisely because they have experienced success and we know success breeds success. More teachers now have a sense of self-efficacy. Many are inviting teachers and classes to hear and evaluate student projects and presentations. I have never been to so many student presentations in all my years at Farrington, and they keep getting better every year.

When we started on this journey, we required teachers to turn in their Quad D lessons on our lesson plan template with student work samples. At the time, the lesson plan template was a way to see how teachers were planning and implementing components of Quad D into the lessons. It also provided me and others an opportunity to provide feedback. However, over time for some teachers, the lesson plan template hindered their creativity. They felt it took too long to fill in the boxes. So this year we provided teachers options to show evidence of Quad D lessons.

Now teachers have a choice of turning in the lesson plan, submitting student work with a reflection, or presenting their Quad D lesson to the faculty. Surprisingly, many teachers have chosen the option to present at the faculty meeting.

The response has been overwhelmingly positive. Teachers are contacting teachers wanting to collaborate on what they saw in the presentations, our faculty meetings are so much more interesting and meaningful, teachers from all disciplines including Special Ed, ELL, PE, and art are teaching others what Quad D looks like across the content areas and empowering teachers to create more engaging, relevant, and rigorous lessons for students. Finally, it reinforces and makes the principal's vision for a Model School a reality.

When the Teacher Leadership Cadre (TLC) began three years ago, it coincided with the start of Quad D training. Together, it solidified teacher collaboration as a way we do things at Farrington High School. Many pieces were in place; teams had some prior experience with collaboration. We started slow, with safe activities: teachers reading articles and discussing it with mixed groupings; we did some inter-rater reliability sessions with anonymous student work to more formal structures like data teams.

We attended an ICLE training by Sue Szachowicz, formal principal of Brockton High School, where she talked about a system where teachers conducted their own professional development. Since we had Jessica Kato, a former teacher at Brockton and now a leader at our school, we knew this was something she could support and lead. We also felt our school was ready for it. There were things we agreed would be non-negotiable:

- PD would be weekly.
- Teachers who wanted to be on the cadre would have to apply.
- Teachers would be paid.
- Team-building would be an important part of the professional development.

Our TLC supported the rigor, relevance, and student engagement efforts in many ways. The cadre used the parts of the CIR rubric to conduct learning walks; they also focused topics on rigor—academic discussion and high-level questions—in their PD sessions, and the collaboration in the weekly sessions made collaboration in other areas such as working on Quad D lessons and WASC focus groups a breeze.

We are nearing the end of our third year of TLC and work with ICLE on designing Quad D lessons. Things are definitely moving from compliance to buy-in. Teachers are asking for time to collaborate within and across disciplines. The lessons keep getting better and better. The faculty sharing sessions have had a positive effect on the culture of our school. It is breaking down the silos by showing all the great things happening in the classrooms and opens the doors for more collaboration. We believe that, as our culture moves from compliance to commitment, as we see more rigorous and relevant instruction and higher student engagement, we will continue to see increased student success.

Can you tell us why you think empowering teachers is so important?

Empowering teachers tells them that you respect their expertise and believe in them. Too many times, we have state/districts and consultants coming into schools telling teachers what they need to teach. It's like discounting all the expertise you have in the building. When you give teachers freedom to design their own professional development for their colleagues, you are sending a strong message to them that you trust them and that will change the culture in your building immensely.

Along with empowering teachers, you also need to give them time to build relationships in order to collaborate on what is important. Just empowering them will not work unless you take the time to build relationships and build their teams. This will lead to productive collaboration, which will in turn lead to teacher efficacy and thriving classrooms.

Many school leaders find it hard to delegate important professional development decisions to others. Can you think of specific examples of how you've released control to the Farrington staff?

First, we used to monitor teacher collaboration when they were developing their curriculum maps, starting PLCs, and working on common lessons. Today, we do not have to do that. Teachers request for days to collaborate and work and we just let them go. Second, the Teacher Leadership Cadre, TLC, was something I certainly could guide or be a part of leading. But I chose not to because I believe that giving them ownership is the only way to truly empower teachers.

Finally, last year's WASC Self-Study was truly a collaborative effort. Department heads were responsible for various random groups. Teachers responded to questions and were responsible for editing each of the sections. Their responses were submitted to the Self-Study for printing.

What advice would you give other schools who are trying to build better teacher collaboration?

- There will be pushback. Be sure you are willing to stay the course.
- Start with something safe and continue to build relationships. This stuff takes time.
- Develop norms and ground rules. Hold people to them.
- Have a purpose for collaboration and a goal in mind.

Table 8.1.   Strategies for Building a Positive Culture

Strategy: *Empower Others*
Cindy Werkmeister, Strategic Planner

This strategy links to the following brain-based research from the chemistry of culture characteristics in chapter 3:

1. Show vulnerability.
2. Release control.
3. Create "challenge stress."
4. Recognize excellence.
5. Share information broadly.
6. Intentionally build relationships.

Farrington's TLC and NTP are powerful models of collaboration and empowerment because they involve and reinforce all six of our brain-based culture characteristics.

Step 1	**Reflect on why it is important to plan strategically for staff collaboration.** The key word here is *strategically*. A culture based on teacher/staff collaboration is one that requires trust. Trust is earned. To build trust well, you need to be sincere, intentional, and strategic. Just because people work together and are polite and friendly doesn't mean they are willing to work collaboratively. When you ask teachers to share the great things happening in their classrooms, you may be surprised to find out how many of them may not want to share. There are many reasons for this. In Hawaii, we live in a culture where "tooting your own horn" is looked down upon. There may just be people who feel they worked hard for what they have and are just not willing to give away what they created, kind of like the aunt who doesn't want to give away her secret recipe. Finally, there is a vulnerability associated with sharing your work. Although you don't expect everyone to be perfect (no one is), there is a sense that teachers are expected to produce quality results for every student. To share your work means you are putting yourself out there for criticism. And although *all* teachers have students who do well, there are also some who do not. I think when teachers share, they fear judgment. Therefore, it is important to keep these things in mind when you are planning for staff collaboration. Creating a safe environment for collaboration takes time, but once teams feel safe, collaboration will begin to grow. It may require a lot of monitoring in the beginning, but eventually it will become part of the culture and teams will thrive.

Step 2   **Plan three staff collaborations.**

1. Reflect on the level of collaboration you want to have for your school. What does that look like? Sound like? Feel like? Once you have a vision for that, assess where your school is now and estimate how long it will take you to get to your desired state. Are you willing to go all in for the long haul? It may take longer than you expect, but don't get discouraged; stay on course. Teams will go through storming phases and it can get ugly but don't give up.

2. Understand Bruce Tuckman's Phases of Teaming. Be willing to work through the storming phase.

3. Establish norms together for working together and use them! Be willing to gently call people on them. Bring them out before every meeting where teachers collaborate.

4. Always start collaboration with a team-building activity. It is so important, especially in the beginning, but also throughout the process.

5. Be cognizant of how you group people. You need some high performers to find value in the work so others can follow. Don't be afraid to group the negative people together. You know your staff best, so you should take some time to determine groups. In the beginning this may take some time, but once people get used to collaborating, it won't matter who sits with whom.

6. When you start with the content, start with something safe. For example, have teachers read an article and have some discussion questions around the reading or watch a video and comment on it. If you want to look at student work, do not use work from people in the building unless they volunteer and are willing to have people take it apart. The NAEP website has student work, rubrics, and ratings that you can use.

7. Depending on what your goals for collaboration are, start introducing them into the process. For example, some of your goals might be developing lessons together and looking at student work together or looking at state test data together and determine where students need help so teachers can discuss how they are teaching it and assessing these areas, or it could be one teacher who needs help on one part of a lesson and others on the team can give suggestions. Ultimately, the goal should be improving student achievement. Whatever your goal is, using protocols is helpful. This website has many to choose from: www.schoolreforminitiative.org/protocols/.

(continued)

Table 8.1. (*continued*)

Step 3	**Monitor your plan.**

There are several ways to monitor collaboration.

1. First, determine your ultimate goal and start with that. Then break down the goal into manageable chunks and backward map. Set quarterly or semester goals; review and adjust as needed.
2. Being there when collaboration is going on is always helpful. In the beginning, it is important and may require you to put all groups in one space so the teams leading the collaboration can roam the room and answer questions or assist as needed.
3. You can require collaborative teams to turn in lesson plans, student work, or minutes.
4. Ask for feedback from teachers.

Whatever you decide on, don't make it part of what teachers do already. You do not want to add to the workload because this could be counterproductive. Eventually, you will need to trust that the teachers will make this a part of the culture.

Step 4	**Review and reflect on your plan.**

Begin by reviewing your plan. What went well? What will you do differently?

Step 5	**Revise your three plans and/or create a new one.**

After reviewing each of the six steps in your three plans:

1. Will you continue? Why or why not?
2. What changes will you make going forward?
3. What will you do differently next time?

Chapter 9

Celebrate Collaboration

Jessica Kato was Farrington High School's Teacher Leadership Cadre and NTP Facilitator, Instructional Coach, and ELA teacher from the beginning of their Model Schools journey. In those roles, Jessica was an instrumental instructional leader whose "disposition for taking action" helped transform the school's culture.

Jessica is important to our story because she can also close another link in our circle of A'o. You see, Jessica came to Farrington by way of Brockton High School in Brockton, Massachusetts, where she got her first teaching job. While at Brockton, she worked with ICLE senior fellow Sue Szachowitcz, along with Maria Lefort and Penny Alschule. These visionary educators recognized Jessica's potential and provided her with many opportunities to learn and grow.

Like many of you, Jessica Kato always wanted to be a teacher and told me emphatically she always knew she would be one. She said that was because as a child she loved books, loved learning, and loved telling people what to do! Jessica was the oldest of three with two younger brothers and liked to "play school" and teach them so many things, her version of a story I've often heard from other teachers.

Growing up, every job she had was working with kids: she taught CCD (religion classes) in her Catholic high school, was a camp counselor and babysitter, and even had a job where she just drove a kid to school each day. In college she was the director of a day camp. Jessica believes that all of these experiences helped shape the teacher she is today and taught her important fundamentals of teaching: how to stay organized, how to keep people engaged, how to pace out time, and how to speak to a group.

But she believes there were other moments that really defined her.

> One was when I was directing that camp, two brothers in second and fourth grade were dropped off . . . the day after their mother was found dead of a drug overdose. Their aunt said she didn't know what else to do with them. I, barely twenty, was locked in a bathroom with one of the boys, for what seemed like forever, as he wailed. This moment really stuck with me because I was brought up in a classic, loving, middle-class home. And even though my parents were public servants and instilled that value in us, I had never really seen the inequities of our society up close, the uphill battles so many people have to face. But I saw it that day with Corey and Devon.

Jessica also shared another critical experience:

> I was working at a program called Summer Bridge, now Breakthrough, in Providence, Rhode Island. This was another college summer. The program was for at-risk middle schoolers and I taught seventh-grade ELA and Improvisational Acting. The program had a dual mission: to support these young students at a critical time in their development but also to train college students to become empathetic educators with a true understanding of diversity as a strength. I think this was the first time that I was in a place where very few people looked like me. My mentor was a man named Esan Looper, and he taught me how to be comfortable as myself in the classroom. He taught me how to be authentic and how to see the authenticity in others and celebrate that.

Jessica stayed at Brockton High School for four years, teaching ninth-grade Honors and an eleventh-grade inclusion class. She clearly remembers walking into the school on the first day questioning if she had made a mistake. Her questioning continued during lunch when a huge fight broke out and she had no idea what to do. But Jessica says now "that choosing to work at Brockton was one of the best decisions of my career."

> Brockton is where I learned how to teach. I got to observe master teachers and a lot was expected of me. Lesson plans needed to be turned in at the start of each week! It is also where I learned to set boundaries for myself. I lost a student, Andre Stone, in the beginning of my last year there. He was shot in retaliation for something he had done earlier in his life.
>
> He knew it was coming. I remember talking with him about his options, which there were not many because he couldn't leave the state due to the

terms of his parole. He had actually disenrolled in school less than a week before he was killed because it was better for him to take night classes.

Because of this, the school didn't do anything to acknowledge his death and I was furious—I actually stormed into Sue's office (which was really not something that was done) and expressed my dismay. Sue did not change her stance, but she did allow me to take a day to go to his funeral.

It was then that I learned that there are so many forces outside of a school's control, but we still need to get up each day and do our best. I think the next time I went into her office was to tell her I was moving to Hawaii.

Jessica added that at the time, Hawaii was a seemingly random choice. But she now believes it is clearly where she was meant to end up. She had a friend who was moving to Hawaii, so she put in an application and went to a job fair in NYC. She landed in Honolulu two days before school started in 2006 and taught a Reading Writing Workshop class for kids struggling in English. After two years she became the English department head and her first task was to revamp the curriculum.

Jessica facilitated the department discussion, which led to an agreement to divide into teams and write new curriculum. In 2011, with the dawn of the Common Core, she added literacy coach to her job title. In addition to training on the standards, she received a lot of training on facilitation and mentoring. Then, in 2015 the idea for the Teacher Leadership Cadre was born and Jessica was tasked with coordinating that effort, which she believes is the most inspiring work she has done. [1]

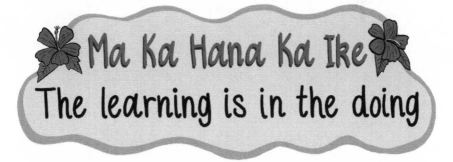

Ma Ka Hana Ka Ike
The learning is in the doing

Interview with Jessica Kato

How has the TLC contributed to improving the culture of learning at Farrington?

I think that TLC has normalized the idea of trying something new in your classroom. Each week we remind the faculty that our goal is to inspire them to experiment with a new strategy, and we build in reflection time each week for teachers to discuss something inspired by TLC they have tried in their classes. Our end-of-year data indicate that 100 percent of teachers tried at least one differentiation strategy from TLC in their classes this year.

To me, this indicates that they are learning and taking risks, which is a culture shift. Additionally, our Learning Group time has created a space for teachers to bring questions to the group and each week multiple teachers have taken advantage of this opportunity. Teachers are feeling comfortable sharing something they need to learn more about and brainstorming ideas with their peers. As a TLC we model lifelong learning, but we also create structures and safe spaces for teachers to explore ideas they want to learn more about.

Has the TLC made a difference for students and, if so, how?

The biggest impact TLC has had on the students is in the quality of instruction they are receiving. Last year, our focus was Project-Based Learning to develop twenty-first-century skills and at the end of the year 91 percent of teachers reported using elements of PBL in their teaching and 96 percent of teachers indicated they focus on at least some twenty-first-century skills.

This year, we worked on differentiation strategies and at the end of the year, 98 percent of teachers reported that they differentiate at least one to two times per week, which is up from just 88 percent, and after TLC, 37 percent indicated they differentiate more than five times a week. Students are being taught the content in a different way and their teachers are getting to know them better, which is resulting in a more personalized learning experience.

What do you think is the TLC's biggest success?

TLC's biggest success is in shifting mindsets to a can-do attitude. Before TLC, it was common to hear excuses about why "our" kids cannot achieve as much as "other" kids. There was also a belief that we need to rely on outside sources to learn strategies and design curriculum. Both of these attitudes have changed dramatically. Teachers are now expecting much more out of their students and are envisioning rigorous Quad D projects for them to work on.

Teachers are believing that their students can take control of their own learning and develop high-level questions and discuss them deeply. And I believe this goes hand in hand with the shift in how teachers are seeing themselves. We no longer look to outside providers for the answers; we look to our colleagues and ourselves. The faculty is proud of the curriculum they designed and wants to share their lessons regularly at faculty meetings. Teachers are willing to take risks, which allows students to be comfortable taking risks, which ultimately creates a culture where all are learning and growing together.

What is one thing you definitely would not try again?

I don't think there is anything I wouldn't try again because we really are an ever-evolving group, so everything we do is born from our previous experiences. A key mistake I made as coordinator in the second year was not laying the right foundation for the TLC. I took for granted our work in year one and overlooked the importance of building trust within the TLC.

We did not read a book together or participate in any kind of community-building retreat; we jumped right into the work and the cracks in our community grew over time and took a lot of work to repair later in the year. But, again, one-on-one conferences with each TLC member grew out of this experience and proved to be so valuable moving forward. I wish they had not been so sorely needed, but the deep reflection that occurred certainly made TLC stronger moving forward.

It's been very inspiring for me to watch Farrington's Teacher Leadership Cadre, or TLC, grow in skill and confidence over the past three years. To do that, I've noticed that your team made adjustments every year. What would you say are the three most important lessons you learned along the way?

TLC began as a simple idea: for teachers to design and facilitate their own professional learning, but as with all visions, once put into practice many details need to be worked out and lessons are learned along the way. We learned a lot from faculty input on how to improve the experience for teachers participating in the professional development workshops, but we also learned a lot about ourselves as leaders and how to function as a highly effective team.

The first lesson was to *clearly define the roles of TLC members and create structures that will ensure the program's longevity.* The first year of TLC was a train charging forward as the tracks were being built just feet in front of it. We were pushing ahead, truly working on adrenaline. The TLC worked well together because we were finding our way together. We did not take the time to clearly define our roles within the TLC or even to nurture our relationships because we did not have the time to stop and think about these things—we were just moving forward, planning and executing professional development.

The toll on the TLC team was not apparent until we moved into our second year and added some new members—that was when the struggle really came into focus. Upon reflection, I realized that there were not enough structures in place to distribute leadership and sustain the program. So we made a few very important decisions. We designed a roles-and-responsibilities document that clearly defined three key roles in the TLC: engaged participant, facilitator, and coordinator.

The engaged participant role description explained the expectations of all TLC members. The facilitator description delineated what the facilitator of each TLC planning meeting should do, and we decided that different TLC members will facilitate each meeting. This decision to rotate facilitators is an important one because it allowed each TLC member the opportunity to meet with me, the coordinator, and plan a TLC meeting. This decision was important because it allowed for me to support and coach the teacher leaders one on one, and it also allowed each TLC member to understand the challenges of facilitating.

The final role we defined is the coordinator role. We documented what the TLC coordinator does each year. This year, I am the coordinator, but by describing the position and not the person, we opened up the possibility that anyone could coordinate moving forward; it is not just one person that drives this mission. We created a structure to distribute leadership and sustain the program.

The second important lesson is to *respond to faculty feedback*. Each year we choose the professional development focus based on a survey given to the faculty. But we also are sure to provide many opportunities throughout the year for the faculty to give us feedback on the workshops we are delivering. The TLC takes these surveys very seriously and reflects on the feedback. There have been some great changes that have come out of this feedback. One was the way we conducted learning visits (which before the feedback we called walkthroughs).

We went through many revisions of the process but ended with a system that provided the teachers choice with who they visit based on a conference-like sign-up system and also a more positive way of providing feedback to those who were visited. We also developed a Learning Group system, which allows for teachers to choose to participate in a Learning Group during TLC time instead of joining the large workshop. In the Learning Group, teachers bring a differentiation question specific to their class and talk through it with a TLC facilitator and other teachers who choose the small group for the session. It is sometimes scary to ask the teachers we work with to give their feedback because it does make the TLC vulnerable to criticism. But it is worth it—we have grown so much by listening to the faculty and making adjustments to improve their experience.

The final, and perhaps most important, lesson is to *continuously build and nurture community and culture*. We always started the year with community builders, but we learned that it is important to continue to do activities that allow faculty to get to know each other on a deeper, more personal level throughout the school year.

We learned that trust is crucial in encouraging faculty to take risks and share about their experiences and also to encourage teachers to try new things. We also really worked hard in the third year to build relationships among TLC members. We started every TLC meeting with a community builder and really cared for our relationships with each other. It is this conscious effort, I believe, that will sustain TLC in years to come.

What advice would give any school wanting to start a process like Farrington's TLC?

Trust and support your team and stay true to the vision. Listen to the faculty you are serving. A Teacher Leadership Cadre is a huge shift in thinking for a lot of people, and with such shifts, there will be struggle. But if you have a core group of teachers who firmly believe in the idea that we can empower each other and learn together, that belief will go a long way.

Make sure the structures are in place to support the system both of the TLC meetings and also of the PD sessions. And, when you plan PD sessions, *plan to inspire*, not to mandate or tell teachers what they must do or how they should be teaching. With this, ask for feedback regularly and listen to it with an open heart. Finally, *be kind to yourself*. This is hard work and it will not always go as planned, but if you stay the course and believe in your school, you will end up in a better place than you started.[2]

Table 9.1. Strategies for Building a Positive Culture

Strategy: *Celebrate Collaboration—Teacher Leadership Cadre*
Jessica Kato, Teacher Leadership Cadre and NTP Facilitator, Instructional Coach, and ELA Teacher

This strategy links to the following brain-based research from the chemistry of culture characteristics in chapter 3:

1. Show vulnerability.
2. Release control.
3. Create "challenge stress."
4. Recognize excellence.
5. Share information broadly.
6. Intentionally build relationships.

The Teacher Leadership Cadre is one of the essential building blocks of Farrington's highly effective culture. As implemented by them, this powerful collaboration strategy links to all six leadership characteristics identified in Paul Zak's neuroscience research. TLC is the weekly process by which they intentionally plan to work on each of the six characteristics.

Every TLC session begins with a relationship-building activity that is carefully planned. Information is distributed. Not just success, but growth and progress are celebrated in a meaningful and intentional way.

In order for professional development to be truly teacher-led, administration must be able to trust and release control. The ability to regularly learn from each other and ask for help requires vulnerability, which is a sure sign of a highly effective culture. Multiple scientific studies show there are few things we can do to more effectively build a positive culture than practice these six characteristics.

Step 1   **Commit to creating a TLC structure.**
- Determine if there will be a compensation schedule for your team.
- Determine how often your team will deliver PD (consistency is key!) and set the calendar.
- Determine how often your teacher leaders will meet to plan; these planning meetings could be paid time outside the school day or take the form of sub days for the teacher leaders to plan.

Step 2   **Create a Teacher Leadership Cadre.**
- Explain the TLC movement to your faculty in a way that empowers teachers to take control of their own professional development.
- Open the application to all teachers in the school. There is a sample application and more resources from Farrington High School in the appendix of this book.
- Choose a diverse team of teachers representing various content areas, years of experience, and philosophies of education.

Step 3   **Support TLC members with a leadership retreat.**
- Retreat should include activities for TLC members to develop trust and collegiality.
- Retreat should include activities to develop norms and decision-making protocols and clarify the various roles within the TLC (engaged participant, rotating meeting facilitator, coordinator).

Step 4   **TLC plans the PD.**
- Survey the faculty to determine the PD focus for the year (TLC can provide four to five options for teachers to vote on).
- TLC planning meetings begin by debriefing previous PD sessions and planning future sessions.
- Each PD session will include: opening time for teachers to reflect on strategies used between sessions, a time to model and practice a new strategy, time to plan forward on how to incorporate new learning in teachers' classes.
- TLC will continuously garner feedback from the faculty and use this feedback in future PD sessions.

Step 5   **Continuously support teacher leaders.**
- The TLC coordinator should have one-on-one check-in conferences with TLC members on at least a quarterly basis.

Notes

1. Learn more about Farrington High School's Teacher Leadership Cadre (TLC) at sites.google.com/farringtonhighschool.org/tlc/home.

2. See appendixes H, I, J, K, L, M, and N.

Chapter 10

Building Better Relationships

We learned in chapter 2 that in the Hawaiian language *Kalihi* means "the edge." Like the tip of a knife blade, Kalihi Elementary School sits at the edge's narrowest point, the tip of the blade, where Kalihi pierces the heart of the Ko'olau Mountains. The school narrows too as it winds through the jungle that stretches up the mountain's side. You have to climb up many flights of switch-back stairs to reach the outer classrooms. Their campus is not for the faint of heart . . . or the short-winded.

But Kalihi Elementary School sits on one of the most beautiful and colorful school locations you will ever see. Kalihi Valley is split down the middle by the Likelike (Lee-Kay Lee-Kay) Highway, with Honolulu off to the east. Looking away from the mountains and back down the valley, the Kalihi neighborhood opens up below you as the knife's edge widens all the way to the blue Pacific, which fills the horizon. The campus setting is stunning. It will take your breath away—literally when climbing to the upper campus!

The history of the community the school serves is just as colorful. Kalihi has a large population of roosters that were once raised for cock fighting. The neighborhood once housed a leprosy receiving station, where suspected leprosy patients were treated before going to the leper colony at Kalaupapa on the island of Molokai. Throughout Hawaii's history, Kalihi has been where wave after wave of immigrants first got a toehold in America. And it still offers some of Oahu's most affordable cost of living.

The Kalihi neighborhood is composed of a diverse collection of hardworking families who take pride in their sense of community. The median household income here is much lower than Hawaii overall, with twice as many people living below Hawaii's poverty level. The vast majority are of Asian ancestry. Tagalog is a hugely important language here, and many Kalihi residents speak it as their primary language. According to www.City.Data.com, about 19 percent of the residents don't speak English well or at all.

Down the mountain and directly across the street from Kalihi Elementary School sits Hawaii's largest Micronesian housing project. And the school's challenging demographics mirror the community.

Kalihi Elementary School Demographics:

- 223 students
- 94 percent Economically Disadvantaged
- 53 percent English Language Learners
- 10 percent SPED
- 43 percent Micronesian
- 29 percent Filipino
- 9 percent Hawaiian

Prior to being named the principal of Kalihi Elementary School, William Grindell served as assistant principal at Farrington High School, where he was an early champion of their rigor, relevance, and relationship work, particularly the relationship part. William instinctively understood the importance of building relationships and was deeply committed to the Farrington culture, having had his first teaching job there. He eventually stayed for ten years in various roles before becoming principal higher up the valley at Kalihi Elementary School, which is arguably the most demographically challenged Farrington High School feeder school.

William spends a lot of time in classrooms, and he immediately connected with the staff during his regular classroom observations. They were impressed by his passion for the students, school, and the Kalihi community. He is a student of Hawaii's history and geography. He spends his free time exploring Oahu on hikes to waterfalls that are sometimes off the regular tourist path. He has learned how to identify kukui nut, breadfruit, and mango trees. He can show you where the real "Gilligan's Island" is located, just off shore near his home by Kaneohe Bay, on Oahu's windward, or wet, side. Once the location for the TV show's exteriors, Coconut Island, as the locals call it, is now home to the Hawaii Institute of Marine Biology. It was on one such hike through a tropical rainforest that William explained how he came to be in this place.

Growing up, my family moved several times before I had graduated from high school. My family and I had lived in Texas, Hawaii, New Mexico, and California. Although I enjoyed living in each of these states, I always knew I would return to the Island of Oahu in the state of Hawaii. When I graduated college, I instantly applied for teaching jobs on Oahu. I convinced my fiancée, who had never been to Hawaii, that although neither one of us had family living in the state, Hawaii was still the best place to raise our future family.

Hawaii is such an amazing place to work and live. My wife and I have never regretted our decision to move here. The best part of living in Hawaii is not the weather or the beaches as many who have not been here believe. The best part of living in Hawaii is the people. I have never lived or visited a place where the people are as welcoming and community-focused as they are in Hawaii. This is also what makes working in education in Hawaii so rewarding: the students, their families, and the school staff all working together for the betterment of the local community.

When William was named principal of Kalihi Elementary School, he knew the rigor, relevance, and relationships work we had started at Farrington was exactly what the school needed. And he decided to start, just like we did at Farrington, with relationships. He understood that meant building trust, collaboration, and empowerment with his staff and students. He began by bringing the staff together to collaborate on the creation of a new vision/mission: "Strengthen Our Community: Develop productive citizens, equipped with the skills needed to thrive in an ever-changing world." The Kalihi mission became "Through intentional actions, we empower individuals to make good decisions, solve problems, and show respect."

Knowing the importance of putting healthy relationships first, he set out to be intentional in creating, maintaining, and monitoring the positive relationships his students have with the adults on campus. That led to the idea of his relationship book strategy. And this strategy is not used in isolation at Kalihi. As William explains, "We utilize many relationship-building strategies including being mindful about keeping a smile on our face, greeting all students at the door every day, standing near the door at the end of the day to say goodbye to every student, and having community circle time established in every classroom."

Since Principal Grindell began intentionally building relationships, he has used multiple strategies, including the relationship book at the end of this chapter. The result is a dramatic and measurable improvement in the school culture of Kalihi Elementary School. Since 2015, Kalihi has seen what may be the most significant improvement of their school culture in all of Hawaii, as measured by the state's annual School Quality Survey, or

SQS. Hawaii uses the SQS to conduct yearly surveys of students, staff, and community. Kalihi Elementary School has seen a significant decrease in behavioral referrals and a huge increase in teacher satisfaction and has doubled the number of third graders reading on grade level.

The number of positive teacher responses to the involvement/engagement questions of Hawaii's School Quality Survey has jumped from 47.7 percent in 2015 to 95.7 percent in 2018. Kalihi's 95.7 percent contrasts dramatically with the state average of 74.7 percent. Teacher satisfaction has gone from just 53.7 percent in 2015 to 88.4 percent in 2018. Again, Kalihi's 88.4 percent compares to the state average 75.1 percent. What's even more impressive is that while Kalihi Elementary School's SQS data have been significantly improving over the past three years, the average SQS data for all schools in Hawaii have been declining.

The full State of Hawaii School Quality Survey data can be found in the state's STRIVE Department of Education report at: www.hawaiipublic schools.org/ParentsAndStudents/EnrollingInSchool/SchoolFinder/Pages/ Kalihi-Elementary.aspx.

Kalihi Elementary School
School Quality Survey Results 2015-2018

SAFETY POSITIVE RESPONSES			
	2015	2017	2018
Teacher	55.8%	77.2%	77.8%
SATISFACTION POSITIVE RESPONSES			
	2015	2017	2018
Teacher	53.7%	86.3%	88.4%

WELL-BEING POSITIVE RESPONSES			
	2015	2017	2018
Teacher	61.3%	92.0%	94.6%
INVOLVEMENT POSITIVE RESPONSES			
	2015	2017	2018
Teacher	47.0%	89.0%	95.7%

Survey Response Rate = 100%

Interview with William Grindell

The relationship book seems like such a simple idea. How do you think it has helped the culture of your school?

For the past several school years, we have focused on the importance of building and maintaining healthy relationships across campus. We had utilized many simple strategies such as greeting each student at the door of the classroom every morning, encouraging staff to smile every day, starting faculty meetings with inclusion activities, and facilitating community circles in every classroom a minimum of one day per week. Though we had some schoolwide data to show we were making progress in the area of positive relationships, the relationship book was a game changer as it had the key elements of student voice and provided instant feedback to each and every adult on campus.

The relationship binder is reviewed by and is accessible to every adult on campus. When reviewing the binder, one cannot help but reflect upon why they may have been identified by a student, why they would identify them as the person on campus they trusted the most, or reflect on why some students have only one or two adults on campus they feel comfortable turning to for support on campus when needed. This information also helps us as the school to identify students in need of more adult connections so we can specifically work on fostering positive relationships with these students.

The book must have seemed threatening to some on your staff. How were you able to get them to go along?

This was something I was concerned about when I proposed the idea to a small team of teachers and our school counselor at a meeting in which we were brainstorming ideas on how we could strengthen our school's positive behavioral support systems. Despite my initial concerns, this small group of teachers became excited about the idea, and as a team we developed what the relationship binder would look like and how we would roll it out schoolwide.

Once we had our plan, we presented it to the entire staff. After this presentation, there were no concerns brought up from any of the staff, and in fact all were in support of moving forward with collecting the relationship information from all students. I believe the reason the staff was not threatened by the relationship binder was because developing and maintaining positive relationships continues to be an explicitly stated focus since I became principal of Kalihi Elementary School, and the entire staff knows the importance positive relationships have on providing our students with the highest-quality learning environment.

Since we have maintained this focus for multiple years, the staff knew the relationship binder was not a mere popularity contest but an extremely valuable tool we could use to collect data needed to evaluate the effectiveness of our efforts as we continue to maintain our positive school culture. We have also spent a lot of time as a school in developing trust among one another, and this trust was extremely important both in collecting accurate and honest information from students and in analyzing this information openly as a school faculty and staff. All of this falls right in line with our school's vision to "Strengthen our Community."

What outcome surprised you the most?

When I looked through the first relationship binder we created, I was pleasantly surprised to see how many students had identified a member of our school's support staff such as our school custodians or members of our cafeteria kitchen staff as one of their key adult relationships on campus. It was also great for these staff members to see this information as it reinforced how important it is for everyone on campus to work together to build and maintain our positive school culture and climate.

Once several months had gone by since we had completed the first relationship binder, I had my next big surprise when I realized just how often I had been utilizing the relationship binder in my interactions with students. I come back to the binder time and time again to look up who on the school staff individual students have identified as being their key adult relationship on campus. Then, as needed, I ask these adults for information, advice, or assistance when I am providing students with support for both minor and major issues.

What advice would you give to those readers who might want to try this strategy?

I would tell them that the relationship binder is a powerful tool for measuring student and adult relationships throughout campus. It can provide specific information to school personnel they can use as they reflect on their own efforts to build positive relationships with students, and it is a valuable resource for counselors and administrators to turn to when they are looking to provide support to individual students. However, as amazing a tool as the relationship binder may be, it is not something you can implement on its own without having some key foundational items in place first.

I believe there are three foundational pieces required for proper implementation of the relationship binder. If your school does not already have these three items in place, I would recommend you establish them before attempting to collect student information for the relationship binder.

First, provide the school faculty and staff with information on the importance healthy student and adult relationships have on developing and maintaining a positive and safe school culture. It is only after the faculty and staff understand why healthy relationships with students are important that they will see the value in creating the schoolwide relationship binder.

Second, I recommend selecting some proactive relationship strategies that will be implemented by all faculty and staff schoolwide. As mentioned earlier, Kalihi Elementary School has agreed as a faculty and staff to greet all students at the door every morning and to try our best to smile more when interacting with students, and all teachers have agreed to spend time once per week facilitating a community circle in their classroom with a purpose of promoting a safe and positive classroom environment.

By setting the expectation of all faculty and staff implementing key relationship strategies schoolwide, you are reinforcing the importance of relationships in building and maintaining a positive school culture. You are also providing an opportunity for faculty and staff to foster positive relationships with students through the use of these strategies before you begin to collect relationship data from students.

The third foundational piece needed for successfully creating a useful schoolwide relationship binder is to ensure you have a culture of trust among the faculty, staff, and students. This trust will enable students to be honest in identifying who they have positive relationships with. The trust among faculty and staff will enable them to openly examine, reflect on, and build upon the relationships or lack thereof that are identified by all of the students they interact with on campus.

In order to establish and maintain trust among the staff at Kalihi Elementary School, we regularly come together during designated professional development meetings to actively engage in team-building activities. During these same meeting times, we also regularly analyze schoolwide data and focus on finding ways to improve upon areas of concern without pointing fingers or assigning blame.

Once the faculty and staff have trust in the fact that the information gathered in the relationship binder will be used to support all students schoolwide as well as to help build and maintain a positive school culture, there will be less of a fear from the faculty and staff that the information gathered will be utilized in a manner to single out individual staff members in a negative way.

When all three foundational pieces are in place, you will be ready to start collecting the information from your students to create your school's first schoolwide relationship binder. Once you have it in your hand, you will find what a valuable tool it is in helping to create, strengthen, and maintain a positive school culture.

Your school campus sits right next to what may be the largest Micronesian community in America. What else have you done to build relationships with them?

At Kalihi Elementary, we use multiple approaches to reach out to and build relationships with all members of our school community. We know that communicating about what is happening at school on a daily basis is an important step in fostering positive relationships with all families. Because of this, we intentionally send out school communications in various forms. As most schools do, we regularly send out schoolwide newsletters with current information regarding what is happening within the school and in each grade level. Knowing that not all of our families are able to read the newsletter, which is written in English, we include pictures of projects, student work, activities, etc. so that students at every grade level can help explain to their parents what is going on in the picture even if they themselves may not be able to read the text.

In addition to the schoolwide newsletter, Kalihi Elementary School is active on various social media platforms and regularly posting images and videos showing what is or will be occurring on campus so that families are aware. When possible we do have written information translated into various languages spoken by our students and their families, including several languages used by our Micronesian families.

Some of the other things we do to build relationships within our greater school community is to host events for parents and community members at our school. On many Sundays, we rent our school cafeteria to a church with a large Micronesian congregation. We have also partnered with community organizations for the past two years to provide parenting classes where we help families who may be unfamiliar with how to support their children at school and at home. These parenting classes help support our families who may not have had much exposure to what our local public school system expects of students and their families. At important parent/student meetings, we offer translators to parents who speak a language other than English.

We also provide opportunities for all students to participate in cultural performances through our school's May Day Program, in which we celebrate the make-up of different cultures represented in Kalihi Elementary School. This event is by far our most attended schoolwide event with parents and other community members often outnumbering the total student population of our campus. At this event, every student participates in culturally relevant performances. In the past several years, our student performances included traditional dances, chants, and practices from Hawaii, Samoa, Chuuk, Tonga, Marshall Islands, and the Philippines.

One other unique thing we do at Kalihi Elementary School is what we call our community walks. Twice per year a group made up of volunteered teachers and staff, including office clerks, our health aid, cafeteria staff, and others who work with our students, go door to door in the public housing complex adjacent to our campus. During this door-to-door community walk, we pass out small treats to each household regardless if they have students enrolled in our school. These community walks provide our staff with the opportunity to meet with and talk to our students and their families in their own community outside of school, and this helps to further strengthen the relationships we have built at the school.

What impact has the relationship book had on your students?

I have not asked a student directly how this has impacted them so I do not know how the students feel about the survey other than they appear happy to have this voice given to them as they are able to share who they have positive relationships with. The relationship survey impacts students in ways they may not notice as we educators are able to use the information the students have provided to support them in proactive ways.

Table 10.1. Strategies for Building a Positive Culture

Strategy: *Building Better Relationships* *William Grindell, principal*

This strategy links to the following brain-based research from the chemistry of culture characteristics in chapter 3:
  4. Recognize excellence.
  5. Share information broadly.
  6. Intentionally build relationships.

If we want the relationships in our classrooms and school to improve, we must plan as strategically for our school culture as we do for our budget!

Step 1	• Create a single-page document that includes the name and picture for every adult working on your campus. • It helps for the document to look like a page in a yearbook. • Be sure to include the photos and names of all teachers, educational assistants, office/clerical staff, and custodial and cafeteria staff. • Include on this single page a place to have students put their name and a simple set of instructions.
Step 2	We wanted our students to be honest in completing the relationship survey and not feel obligated or pressured to circle or star the teacher who was administering this relationship survey to them, so we reached out to counselors from other schools in the area as well as staff from the district office who all came to the school on the day we administered the relationship survey. These volunteers came to the school on the day we were going to administer the survey and received information including verbal instructions on the purpose of the survey and how to run the survey with the students.

Step 3   The volunteers went to each class one at a time. The teacher in the room would step out in the hall and the students were given time to complete the relationship survey. This would take about five minutes per classroom. The volunteers would then collect the surveys, thank the students, and move on to the next room. The teacher would step back in and continue with their lesson.

Step 4   Once all surveys have been completed, our counselor organizes all the surveys into binders. Because we have a smaller school, we have two binders: one for grades K–2 and one for grades 3–5.

Step 5   These relationship binders are stored in a secure yet common place all teachers and support staff have access to. In our case, we keep them in our data/articulation room. The teachers, counselor, support staff, and administrators regularly review the binders. This helps them reflect on their interactions with students. These binders are also excellent resources to utilize when particular students are having a difficult time, are upset, or are dealing with social or emotional difficulties. If the counselor or administrator is working with the student and they are unable to help the student work through the situation because they are not able to make the personal connection at that time, they can refer to the binder and ask for assistance from the adult on campus that the student trusts.

Step 6   We complete this relationship survey at the end of the first quarter of each year and compare students' responses from the previous year to assess if we are successful in developing more positive relationships throughout campus and also to identify students with few or no positive adult relationships so that we can be intentional in supporting these students and fostering positive relationships for them so that they do not slip through the cracks.

Exercise Empathy

Baby Steps . . . Baby Steps

Empathy is emotional metacognition! And in the same way that we can use strategies to increase the metacognition of our students' thinking, there are strategies we can use to increase our students' social-emotional skills such as empathy. It all comes down to practice; in other words, exercise. Use it or lose it. To put it simply, empathy is like a muscle that grows stronger with exercise but withers without it. The brain research that we explored in chapter 3 of this book shows the connection between culture and the chemicals in our brain, and both neuroscience and social science show that we can increase our students' empathy by regularly exercising it. If you need an example, look at Denmark.

Year after year, Denmark is consistently recognized as one of the happiest countries in the world by the World Happiness Report, which ranks 155 countries by their happiness levels.[1] The World Happiness Report was first published in 2012, in support of the United Nations High Level Meeting on happiness and well-being and is considered a landmark survey of the state of global happiness. Every year Denmark ranks in the top three on all the measures found to support happiness: caring, freedom, generosity, honesty, health, income, and good governance. Meanwhile, the United States has never managed to reach the top ten.

Denmark was recently voted number one again in 2018. Why? It can't be the weather. One reason cited by researchers is the emphasis on empathy that the Danes include in their schools. Believe it or not, in Danish schools exercising empathy is thought to be as important as teaching math and literature; and the Danes make sure empathy is part of every child's school curriculum from pre-K through high school.

The Danes understand that empathy plays a key role in improving our interpersonal relationships and contributes to not only our individual happiness but the overall happiness of our society also. When will America begin to recognize that the extreme emphasis on testing and accountability in American schools may come with a considerable cost?

In chapter 4 of this book, we explored the dramatic decline of interpersonal and emotional skills in our culture, which may be associated with increasing rates of anxiety, depression, and suicide among our young people reported in the media. There is no longer any question that we face an unprecedented opioid epidemic as too many of us choose to self-medicate.

There certainly are no silver bullets to solve these problems, but maybe we can learn something from the Danes. Empathy is a learned skill that too many American children are simply not taught. Again, as we learned in chapter 4, multiple studies show empathy levels have dropped between 40 and 50 percent in just the past thirty years, and many social scientists say we have a narcissism epidemic. Here are two proven strategies from the Danish schools that we could use to combat this growing problem.

Step by Step

All Danish children participate in a mandatory national program called Step by Step. Starting in preschool, Danish students are explicitly taught how to recognize and interpret a wide range of emotions such as sadness, anger, fear, frustration, joy, and happiness. In one activity, they are shown pictures of children who are exhibiting a different emotion. With the teacher's guidance, they talk about the pictures and are asked to verbalize what the child is sensing and/or feeling. In this way, they learn to better recognize and understand their own feelings and the feelings of others.

In Step by Step activities, they are exercising empathy while also learning problem-solving, self-control, and how to read facial expressions. These are valuable social-emotional skills that are used to build a better, happier school culture.

2. Klassen Time

Another intriguing program in Danish schools is called Klassen Time, or "Class's Hour" or "the Class Hour cake" in English. Once a week, students bring in a traditional Danish cake that students take turns baking for the occasion and spend an hour interacting with each other. The "Class Hour cake" is such a common part of school culture in Denmark that it has its own recipe.

Class's Hour is focused on helping the children learn to put themselves into each other's shoes. It allows them to build better relationships and to also talk about any problems they may have with each other in school or at home. In addition, teachers often bring up issues they have observed. They try to make sure that the children understand how the other feels and try to come up with a solution together, based on active listening and mutual understanding. Meanwhile in America, many schools struggle to find time even for recess.

But some American schools are beginning to take notice. They have discovered that the Second Step Program for elementary and middle schools is an excellent resource closer to home. Second Step is an innovative social-emotional learning (SEL) program that can help schools build more empathetic, supportive, and successful learning environments.[2] Second Step's comprehensive approach can provide any school with the tools and resources to take a more proactive role in improving the social-emotional growth of all our students. The Second Step Program was created by the Committee for Children, a non-profit organization whose goal is to ensure that all children are emotionally and socially prepared.[3] The Committee for Children has helped pioneer social-emotional learning (SEL) curricula in America.

There is a growing consensus among school leaders about the need to support students in the development of social and emotional skills. It is not a stretch to see that before long SEL requirements will become part of some state assessments. Make no mistake, this book is an attempt to make a case for why schools must now turn their attention to these issues and also increase our sense of urgency about providing school leaders and teachers materials they can use to meet this challenge.

One such resource is *Humanizing the Classroom: Using Role-Plays to Teach Social and Emotional Skills in Middle and High School*, by Kristen Stuart Valdes. Teachers will find many model lessons that are age and culturally appropriate for both middle and high school classrooms. *Humanizing the Classroom* presents a strong argument for using role-plays to teach social and emotional skills and addresses the importance of the how, why, and what of teaching social and emotional skills in our increasingly diverse society.[4]

One reason the culture at Farrington High School is so warm and welcoming is not just because it's located in Hawaii, home of the famous Aloha Spirit. Yes, that fact most certainly gives them a definite cultural advantage. And, yes, all those palm tree–lined beaches don't hurt. But Farrington's real advantage comes from their daily exercise of empathy. At Farrington, the

Aloha Spirit is not just a marketing slogan for the tourists; for much of the Farrington staff it is a mantra. And a mantra is a reminder. It reminds them to practice and to exercise empathy.

To be clear, when it comes to building a positive culture, there is something meaningful, powerful, and useful that those of us on the mainland can learn from Hawaii. There are new data arriving daily from neuroscience, and all the social sciences, telling us clearly that we have a serious and rapidly growing social-emotional problem on our hands, and we need this example more now than at almost any point in a long, long time.

Maybe you've got a classroom full of students or a staff of teachers that are, shall we say, resistant to the concept of empathy? If that's the case, they're the ones that may need it the most. So how do you start? Baby steps, baby steps. But start. Start slow. And make it fun! Hold that thought; we'll return to it shortly.

Empathy is emotional metacognition.

Because the empathy data we reviewed in chapter 4 presents such a compelling call to action, in this chapter we're going to break the pattern we've established so far for how each new strategy is presented in part II. This chapter is structured a little differently. We're going to emphasize empathy by doing a little emotional metacognition. You see, neuroscientific research has uncovered the fact that our brains are hardwired to focus faster on the variation in a pattern. And this is that.

Millions of years of evolution conspire to cause our brains to love, and remember, variety. In this chapter, we'll break the established pattern of the introduction, interview, and strategy template format. We're going to jump right in and explore multiple strategies and links to strategies you can use to exercise empathy. Yes, there are about a million empathy exercises out there that you can Google (and please do). But you're here now, and these are fun. They can be used with both students and adults. Think of it as sort of a strategy bonus.

Now back to that slow start . . .

Maybe a good way to start slow is with something easier for your students or teachers to understand, like their own emotions. Before we can understand the feelings of others, we must deeply understand our own. Exercising empathy starts with self-empathy, and self-empathy is the ability to accurately experience and understand our own emotions. But that's not as easy as it sounds for this totally wired generation.

True empathy connects our emotions to the feelings of others. But in order to do that, we must first be able to be aware of and in tune with our own emotions. Science says too many people are not. The pace of our contemporary culture is hectic, frenetic, crammed, and cluttered! We are constantly bombarded with information and sensations. The pace of life today can sometimes make it hard for us to empathize with those around us. The result is that we don't always take the time to really experience our own emotions in a meaningful way.

This is another example of another reason that the arts can be so valuable in our schools. You don't have to be trained as an actor or author to borrow from their toolbox. Maybe you had a college course in theater or have worked on a school production. Is there someone on your campus who has? If so, they may be able to help explain that one of the first and most important tools actors must learn is observation. Actors are trained to be keen observers of the human condition and are trained to study other people closely, both their physical and emotional characteristics.

By following Shakespeare's "To thine own self be true" advice, we see that often starts with self-study. Actors are taught mindfulness and how to monitor their emotions. Theater and/or acting training can help you find fun ideas and we'll draw on it now for the first few empathy exercises. They are simple variations of basic acting exercises but can be used by anyone to build better relationships and increase empathy.

OK. Some of you have been flipping through this chapter and thinking that this is all a little too touchy-feely for you. So will some of your students and staff. Just remember that, like physical exercise, the ones who are the most out of shape will resist it the hardest. So start slow. But start. Because it can make all the difference for your culture.

Remember that every strategy in part II of this book can be used with both students *and* staff, in the classroom or whole school. Every professional development session at Farrington High School is designed and led by teachers from their Teacher Leadership Cadre. And every one of these PD sessions begins with a quick, fun, relationship-building, empathy-exercising activity.

I believe empathy is the most essential quality of civilization.

—Roger Ebert

Empathy Exercise #1: Self-Empathy

This simple exercise can help students and teachers to identify their own emotions first, which is a good way to start making it easier to empathize with others. It begins with a basic mindfulness technique that can also help us center and calm our emotions.

How to Do It

Ask your students to stand. Encourage them to find a comfortable stance with arms at their side because they should not move and should remain still throughout. When everyone is in position, ask everyone to close their eyes. No talking. No moving. It may take a minute for the energy to settle. Adults can take longer.

Next, ask them to breathe slowly but deeply in and out. Inhale and exhale. Have them pay attention to each breath. Do this for at least a minute, longer for more experienced or receptive groups.

Now, with eyes still closed, ask them to focus on how or what they're feeling. Ask them to monitor their own emotions. You may want to prompt them with a question or not. When some sound or noise in the room takes their thoughts away, ask them to return to their emotions, what they're feeling now, or the emotions they brought into the room. Do this for two to five minutes depending on the group.

Empathy Exercise #2: The Mirror

Exercise #2 can be done following or in connection with Exercise #1. But this exercise is going to be done in pairs and will require more space to spread out and move around.

How to Do It

Start by asking your students to stand. Have them pair up with someone they don't know well. Ask the pair to move to a space in the room where they can stand facing each other and with enough room for them to circle each other. When everyone is in position, ask them to face each other. Have them decide who will be the observer and who will be observed.

Next, the observed person stands relaxed, with hands down at sides. Observer moves around the other person as much as possible and observes the person closely from all angles. Have them observe the posture, stance, arms, hands. Make mental notes of the smallest details for two to three minutes.

Now ask the observer to "mirror" the person they were observing as closely as possible. Their goal should be to mirror or copy what they observed as closely as possible. The facilitator should move around the room and give feedback to each pair. Did they get the feet right? How about the arms and shoulders?

Next, have each pair switch roles and repeat each step. End by asking each pair to share with each other what they observed and what each role felt like for about two minutes. You can roll this up to the whole group by asking for someone to share something they heard (not something they said themself) that they thought was interesting or important. You will find an excellent example of the basic mirror exercise being done with students at this link: www.youtube.com/watch?v=w13LC6DLMn8.

Exercise #3: Synchronized Storytelling

How to Do It

This fun little exercise is a version of the mirror activity above and also requires working in pairs. It's a good one for younger students. One student tells a story while the other person acts as a mirror and tries to follow along, telling the same story at the same time. So, if one says, "Once upon a time," the idea is that their partner is going to follow along, repeating it exactly, as close as possible to the same time. This takes some practice and can be a little slow at first. But it may surprise you. What happens is that the person following the storyteller becomes intently focused on the person telling the story. And because the activity requires almost 100 percent concentration on another person, there is a natural opportunity to practice empathy. Make sure you both have a chance to play both roles and notice:

- Are you thinking of anything besides the person telling the story?
- What hints do you get from the storyteller that don't involve words?
- How does the activity impact your relationship with your partner?
- What is easy and comfortable for you versus what is unfamiliar?

Empathy Exercise #4: From the Actor's Toolbox

Here's another example of a technique that actors learn to understand emotions but can also be used to exercise empathy. It starts by closely observing the physical characteristics of another person and working backward to understand how those outward physical characteristics of the body are connected to the emotions on the inside.

How to Do It

Think of someone you want to empathize with, a friend, a family member, a colleague, or even a romantic interest. Remember a recent interaction you had with this person, especially one that left you confused about how they were really feeling. Now try to imitate, as closely as you can, the physical posture, facial expression, exact words, and vocal inflection they used during that encounter. Pay close attention to the emotions that you begin to experience.

Listen to your body. Whatever you are feeling can help you to get closer to whatever the other person was going through. Often even our deepest emotions have outward, subconscious physical expression. It happens without thinking. Even when we try to hide feelings of anger or frustration, our bodies betray us. We do this naturally whenever we try to read the "body language" of another person.

When beginning work on a new character, many directors will encourage an actor to start from the outside and work their way in. What they mean by this is figure out how to walk, move, sit, or stand like the character you are playing and let that be your guide to their feelings. Because, as neuroscience and psychology confirm, our body shapes itself in response to our feelings.

Shaping our body to match another person's is an excellent way to build empathy. As a result, many actors spend a lifetime reading body language. Think of Meryl Streep, how she disappears into the characters she plays. It's really all about the power of observation. Great actors often become such highly empathetic people that their characters' pain can become their own. In interviews and books, actors often share how difficult it can be to cope with the emotional strain of some roles.

Why Empathy Matters

At the International Center, we believe you should always start with the why. In our coaching work with school leaders and teachers, we model returning to the why often. So, let's return to why empathy matters briefly here. Empathy represents our ability to understand someone else's thoughts and feelings. And as we learned in chapter 4, empathy is a primary ingredient of trust and trust is the foundation of any culture. In that way, empathy has a profound impact on any organization's effectiveness, engagement, and loyalty. How profound?

- Seventy-seven percent of workers would be willing to work more hours for a more empathetic workplace.
- Sixty percent would actually accept a slashed salary for the same.
- Ninety-two percent of HR professionals note that a compassionate workplace is a major factor for employee retention.
- Eighty percent of millennials noted that they would leave their current job if their office became less empathetic. Sixty-six percent of baby boomers also shared this sentiment.

If these social-emotional skills are so important, why don't we spend more time on them in our schools? Well, one thing we know for sure is that there's never enough time! And building a more compassionate and empathetic school culture does take time. But here's something else to consider. As the dramatic decline of empathy among our young people that we explored in chapter 4 becomes more widely known and better understood across our country, how will communities and politicians react? To whom will they turn to solve this problem?

They will turn to us. And there will surely be increasing calls for our schools to exercise empathy. That will mean building better relationships, finding solutions to offset the negative effects of "screen time," and looking for innovative ways for both teachers and students to connect, face to face. That will take planning, budgeting, and scheduling. In other words, a strategic schoolwide effort. The neuroscience and psychological research are clear. By regularly exercising empathy, we can make our school and classroom cultures more positive and effective.

For these reasons, every weekly teacher-led Professional Development Session (NTP) at Farrington High School begins with a relationship-building activity designed to exercise empathy. They do not leave it to chance. Our work with Farrington and their feeder schools, Kalakaua Middle and

Kalihi Elementary schools, has included empathy exercises like the ones above, which are now a part of the culture in these schools. So, let's return to exploring some more ways you can exercise empathy now.

Empathy Exercise #5: Active Listening

Scientists have hard research data to document the decline of empathy in our culture. But they are equally certain we don't listen as well either. And, while we're at it, let's be honest: you know we're not all reading our e-mail either! Experts who study communication confirm that, when a breakdown occurs, when we have a failure to communicate, the problem is not on the sender's side, because they didn't say it clearly or that they just forgot to tell us. No. Truth is, most of the time, the communication breaks down because we didn't read the e-mail or hear what was said correctly. Oh, we listened . . . but we didn't hear. Because we don't practice active listening.

Actively listening to others requires practice. Communication experts have identified five key active listening techniques you can use to become a more effective listener. They are: pay attention, show that you're listening, provide some immediate feedback, defer judgment, and respond appropriately.

1. Pay Attention
Give the speaker your undivided attention and actively acknowledge the message. Recognize that nonverbal communication not only speaks; it sometimes "shouts" loudly.

- Look closely at the speaker by making eye contact often.
- Put aside distracting thoughts.
- Don't be thinking only of how you want to respond!
- Avoid being distracted by outside factors like side conversations.
- "Listen" to the speaker's body language.

2. Show That You're Listening
It's important to intentionally use your own body language, posture, and gestures to show that you are engaged. In other words, lean in.

- Nod occasionally.
- Smile and use other facial expressions.
- Make sure that your posture is open and interested.
- Encourage the speaker to continue with small verbal comments like "yes" and "uh huh."

3. Provide Some Immediate Feedback

As a listener, your role is to understand what is being said. This may require you to reflect on what is being said and to ask questions.

- Reflect on what has been said by paraphrasing. "What I'm hearing is . . ." and "Sounds like you are saying . . ." are great ways to reflect back.
- Ask questions to clarify certain points: "What do you mean when you say . . ." or "Is this what you mean?"
- Summarize the speaker's comments periodically.

4. Defer Judgment

In our increasingly polarized world, this skill is harder to find. You certainly won't see much of it modeled on cable news channels, so just do the opposite of what you're watching.

- Interrupting is a complete waste of time. It frustrates the speaker and limits full understanding of the message.
- Allow the speaker to finish each point before asking questions.
- Don't interrupt with counterarguments.

5. Respond Appropriately

Active listening is designed to encourage respect and understanding. You are gaining information and perspective. You add nothing by attacking the speaker or otherwise putting her down.

- Be candid, open, and honest in your response.
- Assert your opinions respectfully.
- Treat the other person in a way that you think she would want to be treated.

Empathy Exercise #6: Active Listening

How to Do It

This exercise is designed to practice active listening with a partner. It is best done somewhere you can talk comfortably without distraction. One of you starts by sharing a subject of their choice. As they do so, try to follow these steps. You don't need to cover every step, but the more you cover, the more effective this practice is likely to be.

Paraphrase

Once your partner has finished expressing a thought, paraphrase what they said to make sure you understand and to show that you are paying attention. Helpful ways to paraphrase include "What I hear you saying is . . ." "It sounds like . . ." and "If I understand you right . . ."

Ask Questions

When appropriate, ask questions to encourage your partner to elaborate on their thoughts and feelings. Avoid jumping to conclusions about what the other person means. Instead, ask questions to clarify their meaning, such as "When you say_____, do you mean_____?"

Express Empathy

If your partner shares negative feelings, strive to validate these feelings rather than questioning or disagreeing with them. For example, if your partner expresses frustration, try to consider why they feel that way, regardless of whether you think that feeling is justified or whether you would feel that way yourself were you in his or her position. You might respond, "I can sense that you're feeling frustrated" and even "I can understand how that situation could cause frustration."

Use Engaged Body Language

Show that you are engaged and interested by making eye contact, nodding, facing the other person, and maintaining an open and relaxed body posture. Avoid attending to distractions in your environment or checking your phone. Be mindful of your facial expressions: avoid expressions that might communicate disapproval.

Avoid Judgment

Your goal is to understand your partner's perspective and accept it for what it is, even if you disagree with it. Try not to interrupt with counterarguments or mentally prepare a rebuttal while the other person is speaking.

Avoid Giving Advice

Problem-solving is likely to be more effective after both conversation partners understand one another's perspective and feel heard. Moving too quickly into advice giving can be counterproductive.

Take Turns

After your partner has had a chance to speak and you have engaged in the active listening steps above, it's your turn to share your perspective. When sharing your perspective, express yourself as clearly as possible using "I" statements (e.g., "I feel overwhelmed when you don't help out around the house"). It may also be helpful, when relevant, to express empathy for the other person's perspective (e.g., "I know you've been very busy lately and don't mean to leave me hanging . . .").

Empathy Exercise #7: Walk a Mile in Their Shoes

You've heard the old cliché about not being able to really understand another person until you've walked a mile in their shoes. Think back over the past month. Was there a time when someone—a stranger, a friend, maybe someone at work—angered you for some reason? If you reflect back on this situation, some of the original emotions might even come back to you. Try to recall the situation as clearly and unemotionally as you can. Try to remember not only how you felt but also what you thought. What reasons did you tell yourself to justify your behavior?

Now, try to step into the shoes of the person that upset you so much. This will likely be difficult at first but try. Try and put yourself into the shoes of the other person. Try to see the situation from that person's perspective. Give it a little time. Try to separate yourself from whatever opinions you originally had. Note: this is pretty hard for most of us to do. But if more of us got good at it, imagine how much less conflict and drama there would be in our lives.

While you're in this heightened state of open-mindedness, maybe, just maybe . . . you will be able to discover something about the reasons the other person behaved as they did, reasons you had not understood before. You don't have to agree or approve of what they said or did, but by identifying, naming, and possibly understanding their reasons, you will have taken an important step on the path to greater empathy and compassion.

Empathy Exercise #8: Shadow a Student Day

If you've been reading along in this chapter and thinking that some of these exercises might be too touchy-feely for you or your staff, don't worry. That's OK. There's no one right way to exercise empathy. Spend a little time on Google and you will discover activities of all kinds, more than you will ever have time to use. But if you're feeling confident and strong, maybe you ought to try to shadow a student. It can be done by both school leaders and teach-ers. It's simple, but it's a tough one, often hard for those who try to finish.

The "shadow a student" strategy builds on the "walk a mile in their shoes" exercise. Because that is what you do. Pick a student at random. Let them know what you are planning to do and make sure they're OK with it. Meet the student when they first arrive on campus. Think of yourself as that stu-dent's shadow. Try not to interact too much with them. Your task is to follow them throughout the day. Go where they go and do what they do. Shadow them for an entire day.

As you go through the day with your student, continue to try and see the lesson, the class, and the school through their eyes. Try to understand how they feel. Listen to the student you're shadowing and to those around him or her. How does each class look from their perspective? Ask yourself how you would feel in the student's place. How do we fill their time? How are their interactions with others? Is your school's culture regularly bathing their brain in oxytocin?

Some educators who've done this exercise have shared how transforma-tive the experience was, how it changed the way they saw their school and school culture. You may be tempted to think that you don't have enough time to do this. A whole day? That's crazy. But is it crazy to listen to our students—to walk a mile in their shoes?

Notes

1. The World Happiness Report is available at worldhappiness.report/.

2. To learn more about Second Step, visit www.secondstep.org/.

3. To learn more about Committee for Children, visit www.cfchildren.org/about-us/history/.

4. Kristen Stuart Valdes, *Humanizing the Classroom: Using Role-Plays to Teach Social and Emotional Skills in Middle School and High School* (Lanham, MD: Rowman & Littlefield, 2019).

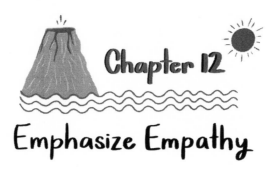

Chapter 12

Emphasize Empathy

If you're now twelve chapters into this book and still wondering what makes the culture of Farrington High School so special, please consider this. Remember how in 2018, the students at Farrington High School made what was maybe their ultimate empathy statement when they introduced Farrington senior Jasmin Cozo as their 2018 Homecoming Queen? You see, Jasmin was born with severe Down syndrome. "Everyone was excited. Her parents were excited. The whole school was excited," said Farrington quarterback Chris Afe. The student body overwhelmingly voted for Jasmin, at every grade level, and she proudly reigned during the entire week-long homecoming festivities. The winning vote came after a campaign by the school's FRIENDz Program, where special needs and general ed students do activities together.

At halftime of the homecoming game, Jasmine and her Homecoming Court took to the field and performed a choreographed dance number. Jasmin says she's happy she was elected as Farrington High School's first special needs Homecoming Queen and that "the dancing was my favorite part."

"We choose to include and break barriers," said Homecoming King Jaymar Enanoria, who seemed incredibly proud of his supporting role. Maybe that's because Jasmin is well liked by her fellow students, and with coaching from the Farrington FRIENDz, she competes, and wins, as a Special Olympics athlete.

High school can be a particularly rough time for many students as they navigate adolescence, try to figure out who they are, and find a place where they can fit in on a large campus. Social media has not made this task any easier for any of them. And it is even harder for any child perceived as "different."

But on most American high school campuses, it is easier for one group. Athletes in general, and football players in particular, often form an exclusive club with a special social status. In many schools, they are some of the most well-known and popular kids on campus. But Farrington High School's football team isn't exclusive; it is inclusive. At Farrington, the football team and other star athletes emphasize empathy.

Starting in 2012, members of the Farrington football team began meeting at lunch with special needs students. Their single goal was to emphasize empathy by building better relationships. But it did not happen by chance. It was intentional and done by design. It was the Farrington High School FRIENDz Program, started by vice principal Ronald Oyama.

The Farrington FRIENDz Program has now grown to more than forty general education students who volunteer to meet every week to make sure that at Farrington, *all* means *all*, that *all* students have the opportunity to participate in *all* that high school has to offer. Since Farrington students are known as the Governors, the FRIENDz motto is "One love, one Gov." There is no stronger manifestation of the Aloha Spirit than the Farrington FRIENDz Program.

Current Louisiana State University Division I football player Breiden Fehoko was one of the first students to help make this special connection. As a nationally recruited high school prospect, Fehoko was a pretty big deal on campus. But he took his leadership role seriously. During his senior year, he and fellow star Bryce Tatupu-Leopoldo used their popularity to help make inclusion cool and emphasize empathy.

Breiden and Bryce decided to take time out from their very busy senior year to team up with Farrington special education advisors Evelyn Utai and John Yago to organize bowling trips, college tours, and friendly football games. That's how Farrington slowly began to not only emphasize empathy but to make it cool. As a result, the FRIENDz Program has led to a better understanding among students and has helped create a culture of acceptance and inclusion for Farrington's Life Skills Special Education students. And Breiden and Bryce left a lasting legacy.

Every school year Farrington's FRIENDz Program takes on the challenge to #BETHECHANGE. Special education students, along with the athletes and general education friends, meet every week during lunch to hang out, play games, and form lasting friendships. Together they plan and execute their very own "FRIENDz Prom!" They work with the school's media program to create videos to spread awareness on how beneficial being an inclusive and unified school can be. Together, they created a schoolwide campaign called Spread the Word to End the R-Word. They held rallies with whole-school engagement activities designed to help general education students empathize with their special education counterparts.

Farrington student athletes also help their friends train for the Special Olympics by dedicating their time to make sure their friends bring home the gold! Recently the National Special Olympics honored the Farrington High School Governors, the Govs, by naming them National Unified Champion School with banners that hang in the gym and at their football stadium.

Unfortunately, you don't have to be a special needs student to have your school experience disrupted and hopes crushed by bullying. Surveys show that one-fifth to over one-half of students in both public and private schools have been bullied or harassed. Even the Aloha State is not immune. But the culture of Hawaii does provide some advantages. The E Ola Pono Program is one.

E Ola Pono

In the Hawaiian language, E Ola Pono means to live with respect for and in harmony with everyone and everything around you. Hawaii's annual state-wide E Ola Pono Campaign challenges students to work together on activities or projects that promote Pono as a "Way to Be." The campaign encourages youth groups to promote peace, Pono, and respect at their schools and communities through student-led campaigns. Student groups are encouraged to actively Grow Pono, to foster respect and harmony.

The E Ola Pono Campaign was created as a cultural response to bullying in the schools and just celebrated its tenth year. Each year six schools in three divisions—elementary, middle, and high—receive recognition and cash rewards for their campaigns. Last year the Farrington FRIENDz Program again won first place in the high school division.

Teachers and school leaders know that bullying has many underlying causes and is often the result of underlying stigma and prejudice. The FRIENDz Program has chosen to move beyond telling students it's bad to be mean and start showing them how they can be empathetic and inclusive.

Kumu Hina

Another great example is *Kumu Hina*, a nationally broadcast PBS documentary about a Native Hawaiian teacher who empowers her students in downtown Honolulu by showing them the true meaning of Aloha. A youth-friendly, short version of the film called A *Place in the Middle* is also available on PBS at no cost for streaming and download from PBS Learning Media and on Vimeo.

The film focuses on the story of a sixth-grade Native Hawaiian girl, Ho'onani, who dreams of joining the boys-only hula troupe. This might make her a prime target for bullying in many schools, but this story has a very different ending. A *Place in the Middle* is a powerful example of why students who are perceived to be different, in one way or another, deserve to be celebrated precisely because of those differences.

You will find a beautiful short video of Ho'onani opening the 2017 Farrington May Day Celebration with a traditional Hawaiian chant at: youtube/4j1sN4tv9Xc.

At a time of deep cultural division in our country, it is encouraging and uplifting to experience Farrington's highly empathetic culture. But just a few years ago Farrington carried the stigma of being a pretty tough inner-city school. But they decided to do something about it. They decided to emphasize and exercise empathy. In so doing they have proved schools can build a better culture for all their students. Today, Farrington has become a bright beacon of hope from which we all can learn. Nowhere in Hawaii is the Aloha Spirit stronger than in the Farrington FRIENDz Program.

Interview with SPED Educational Assistant Evelyn Utai

Can you tell us a little about why you are so committed to Farrington's FRIENDz Program?

The FRIENDz Program gives the students with special needs a chance to experience high school with all the fun of having friends. It gives our general education students a window into just how difficult life is with and without disabilities. It gives them a window to know and appreciate life. I am committed to the FRIENDz Program because I love seeing the change. I've seen one of our shyest students blossom into a social butterfly. I've seen one of our general education students who was known around high school as a gangster, someone who was hard-core and had to be avoided, I've seen him melt and interact with our students and transform his life.

What were some of the biggest barriers you encountered while getting it started?

Like many schools, our first big barrier was funding. One of the important things we decided to do is provide lunch on our program days. We wanted to find a natural way so that we can have our students just get into hanging out with their friends. Our regular lunch lines here at school are long; if our general education students had to stand in the regular line to get their lunch, they would only have about ten minutes to spend with their friends.

A lot of the extra activities, like the Christmas Luncheon, that we wanted the friends to be able to share also need money. Our special education students participate fully in all school activities like prom, Homecoming performances, Friendsgiving, Farrington's Valentine's Day party, and held canned food drives. Our SPED students are included and accepted. I believe the FRIENDz program has helped the general education students to empathize and understand our group.

We also make sure the FRIENDz take field trips to the movies together, to away football games, May Day Performances. Last year Hawaii Congresswoman Tulsi Gabbard came to visit us because we've hosted some of the largest Ban the R-Word campaign rallies in the state. Our students went to the state capitol to rally, and we've had to shuttle sixty-passenger busloads of general education student so they could support their friends who were competing in the Special Olympics.

We believe it's important to take our kids out for outings so that they can experience what it's like to go out with friends. Many of our students come from homes that are already financially struggling, so many of the field trips/outings/lunches are provided by the advisors.

What do you think are a few of the FRIENDz Program's biggest successes?

I can think of three things. First, know it has given our students with special needs more self-esteem. You can see that and feel it. Second, I've seen how it can help change the attitudes of the general education students. And finally, we've created some real bonds between special needs and general education students, bonds that last over time. You can see that when our graduates return to campus.

Long after my work at Farrington is finished, I know that some of my strongest memories will be of activities I've shared with the FRIENDz. For example, the big May Day Show where students from all the islands dress in the traditional clothing of their home and perform a dance from their culture. Without being here, it's hard to fully appreciate what a big deal it is for the students and the community. It's simply the most amazing and inspiring thing I've ever seen in a high school.

Our kids look forward to the May Day Show, what we also call the Founders Day Celebration, all year. Some years we dance as a group, with all the islands represented, and sometimes our students dance with the gen. ed. students from their home island.[1]

I'm thinking about your students performing in the May Day Show. What I remember is how the student body supported and cheered them. I wish the readers of this book could experience a May Day celebration. You have these beautiful island cultures represented—Samoan, Tahitian, Tongan, Micronesian, Philippine, Japanese, Marshallese, Chinese, and of course Hawaiian.

The way they cheer and support each other as they dance is something special. There's a special spirit in the room. And the way all the student groups include and celebrate the FRIENDz is unlike anything I've seen before.

We are blessed.

What would you suggest to any school trying to start a similar program?

I'd say start slow. It takes time to build the relationships naturally. It can't be forced. But if you create the right settings and opportunities, the connections will happen and the relationships will form. Make sure to get administrative buy-in and support. The FRIENDz Program would not exist without Principal Carganilla and VP Ron Oyama. They not only support; they participate. They're always checking on us to make sure we have what we need.

Get support from the general education teachers. Make sure you communicate with them and include them in activities whenever you can. Look for ways to support them. Talk to them and the counselors about general education students who might be a good fit in your program. Look at staff who would support a program or could be recruited. Finally, never stop looking for funding!

Table 12.1. Strategies for Building a Positive Culture

Strategy: *Emphasize Empathy* *Evelyn Utai, SPED Educational Assistant*
This strategy links to the following brain-based research from the chemistry of culture characteristics in chapter 3: 　1. Show vulnerability. 　4. Recognize excellence. 　6. Intentionally build relationships.
Being vulnerable means being open and honest about ourselves, most importantly about our strengths and weaknesses, mistakes and failures. Vulnerability is only found in high-trust teams. Students in high-trust schools can not only acknowledge their weaknesses but also freely ask for help from others. Paul Zak's research team found that this behavior stimulates oxytocin production and increases trust and cooperation. This strategy shows that you can help your teachers and students build better relationships by working on it. There is hard science to say that when a team cares about one another, they perform better. The research findings show clearly that better relationships = more empathy, and more empathy = greater trust. And trust is the foundation of your school or classroom culture.

(continued)

Table 12.1. (*continued*)

Step 1	Find someone who has the heart and passion to champion the program, to put in the time to make it work, someone who believes it is important.
Step 2	Find an administrator to support the program. You need an administrator who believes, who will personally commit support with funding, transportation, and the schedule flexibility needed. Your champion does not have to be an administrator, if they are in a position to leverage the administrative support needed.
Step 3	With your champion's lead, begin to communicate your message of inclusion schoolwide using a variety of methods and media.
Step 4	Recruit well-known and highly visible students from the general education population such as athletes and/or student leaders who will commit to being personally involved with your program. Often, they will not understand the program's value until they experience it for themselves.
Step 5	Build positive relationships with all teachers and staff. Communicate with them regularly about the importance of your program.
Step 6	Celebrate your program's successes regularly.
Step 7	Continue to look for new sources of funding to grow your program.

Note

1. Farrington High School May Day Video Links:

Farrington High School SPED Program Perform for May Day: www.youtube.com/watch?v=oQYLKxsZIqY

Farrington High School [May Day] 2017: Tahiti Performance: www.youtube.com/watch?v=InBksOTsm0c

Farrington High School [May Day] 2017: Micronesia Performance: www.youtube.com/watch?v=DJnU_6plC3s

Farrington High School May Day 2017 (Tonga Section): www.youtube.com/watch?v=nupHFbJy20Y

Farrington High School May Day 2017 "Micronesia": www.youtube.com/watch?v=LvCLKSOND5U

Farrington High School [May Day] 2017: Marshall Islands Performance: www.youtube.com/watch?v=OWhvFKlITDw

Farrington High School May Day 2017 Filipino Performance: www.youtube.com/watch?v=UAu4dFIm1IY

Farrington High School [May Day] 2017: South Korea: www.indosatu.net/video-news/watch/8SMmsGgXYI4/farrington-high-school-may-day-2017-south-korea-kpop-performance/

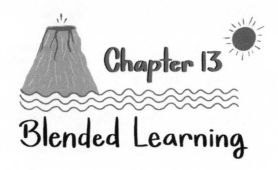

Chapter 13

Blended Learning

In the spring of 2015, Sean Witwer was teaching ninth-grade Algebra in a second-floor room with large, steel-louvered windows, all wide open to catch the trade winds because, like most Farrington High School classrooms, this one had no air conditioning. Sean was not happy. And neither were his students. But it had nothing to do with the lack of air conditioning. At Farrington High School they are used to that.

Sean is an excellent math teacher. He cares deeply about his students and builds strong relationships with them. He knows his subject inside and out. Sean was not happy because he has high expectations and wants his students to learn. Sean worked hard every day to teach them Algebra. But despite his best effort, his students were struggling—and failing. In fact, Sean had the highest student failure rate in the school.

This is a common problem that we see over and over again, in state after state, school after school. Algebra is most often the gateway to either success or failure in high school. It's literally the door through which most dropouts pass on their way out of school, particularly for demographically challenged students like Sean's. We asked Sean what he thought the problem was.

He answered quickly. "They can't do Algebra because they don't know arithmetic. This is the Algebra book I'm given, and I'm paid to teach them Algebra! I can't just give them a grade. . . . I'm as frustrated as they are." His answer did not surprise us.

How many times have you heard a version of this conversation with a math teacher? But what if Sean's mental model of a "good" math teacher could be the problem? Sean's honest self-reflection started him on a four-year journey that goes on to this day, during which Sean has literally re-invented his math class. But it all started with Sean beginning to create a mental model, his own model, of what a "good" math teacher was.

You see, Sean was right from the start. His students didn't know arithmetic. On his own, Sean used multiple placement tests to assess his students. More than a third were not fluent in their basic math facts of addition, subtraction, multiplication, and division. Many were below fourth grade. Worse yet, proficiency levels in a class of thirty students ranged from second to tenth grade.

It was about this time that Farrington principal Al Carganilla was rolling out his "pre-forgiven" mantra in order to build trust and encourage teachers to innovate. Sean began to wonder if the principal was really serious, and what it might mean for him. Ultimately, Sean decided that he would put Principal Carganilla to the test, and this was the perfect opportunity for him to try the things he wanted to explore. In some ways, this was a turning point not just for Sean but for the whole school culture.

Blended learning is a powerful strategy and teaching tool because it allows a teacher to leverage technology to deliver personalized instruction. Through the use of computers, a teacher is able to deliver course content and instruction and differentiate according to the student's needs. In a blended Learning classroom, a teacher transitions from the "sage on the stage" to a "guide on the side" as students are empowered with greater responsibility for their own learning.

Sean Witwer will explain what happened next.

Interview with Sean Witwer

Would you mind telling our readers a little more about your why, more specifically, why you decided to begin your effort to actually "re-invent" how you were teaching math?

I have to make a confession. The first time you talked with me about making changes in my instructional approach nearly four years ago, and the idea of blended learning, I wasn't really receptive to it. I responded as most veteran teachers would, having an "outsider" giving them instructional advice—I respectfully listened to your ideas but never really took them seriously, to the point where I would actually change my instructional philosophy and implement his ideas.

It was probably a combination of things—I was still finding success with the instructional strategies I was using in class, the student demographics I had in class hadn't yet necessitated a change, and, perhaps most importantly, the timing wasn't right.

To understand my initial resistance to your suggestions on implementing blended learning, and how and why I was finally willing to implement it into my classroom practices, it is important to understand a little bit about my teaching journey. For readers who have found success using methods that once proved successful, you may be able to relate to my story.

In 2015, I was a regular education math teacher. Out of the sixty or so students who made it to Calculus at that time, ten of them were once my former students. At our graduation ceremonies, Farrington High School had six valedictorians. Four of them were former freshmen. Based on my informal observations, it seemed that about half of my former freshmen went on to graduate with honors from high school, cum laude or above, that year. In general, I felt content with the success of my students.

However, there were changes happening in the state as far as our math curriculum, and it was beginning to affect the success I was seeing in the classroom. At times I voiced my frustrations to you, and you recommended changes in my instructional approach.

During the second year that you would come to my classroom, things had really begun to take a downward dive. My teaching style, which relied heavily on direct instruction, and the new curriculum were not a good fit. I also felt that the students that were entering my classroom were also not as well prepared for high school as previous classes. The number of students earning Fs in my freshmen class was beginning to increase.

In March of 2016, my principal, Mr. Carganilla, called me into his office. He explained to me that there was a particular shortage of special education teachers and he might need to move me back to the special education department the following school year, since I was dual certified.

That year, because of these and other factors, I thought of leaving Farrington High School and the Department of Education *a lot*! But I decided to stay, and although I initially hated the idea of moving, I decided to make the most of it.

After being a regular education math teacher for eight years, teaching again in the special education department was a hard transition. In regular education, most of my students had at least about fifth-grade skills and above; most of the SPED students I now had were at the second- to fourth-grade level. Teaching out of the Algebra book was painful for me, the students, and everyone involved. It was a disaster, and by the end of my first semester back in special education, I wanted to throw in the towel.

When you continued to come back to visit and talk, I started to become much more receptive to what you were saying. You let me know that Mrs. Sebok, another teacher on campus, was implementing blended learning, and you suggested we go and look at what she was doing.

You and I spent about ten minutes in Sebok's class and I was sold. I loved that students could get targeted math instruction, at their ability level, and I knew that I wanted to implement it immediately.

How did you decide to begin?

Thankfully, our administration was supportive and helped me to get the technological resources I needed right away. Within about a month, I got a new classroom set of Chromebooks and I decided to implement blended learning at the start of my second semester.

The second semester was such a huge turnaround!

Along with the Chromebooks, I also had STAR Math, an online, adaptive assessment program that could immediately give me the grade equivalency data I needed to place the students in the proper curriculum track. Based on their ability level, I either placed my freshmen students in Arithmetic, Pre-Algebra, or Algebra using Khan Academy that second semester.

I can't stress enough how important it was that Principal Carganilla allowed me to have the creative control that I needed in my classes, even to register the students according to their data and needs. I tried to make sure I had the support of key decision makers on campus.

Can you briefly share some of the results of your efforts?

Regarding our results, the students that followed directions, watched the Khan Academy videos, wrote notes daily, and completed the lessons had some amazing results. Many of the students within that second semester had gains of one-, two-, and three-grade equivalency grade levels. Some of my best students had five to seven grade levels in gains, from fifth- to twelfth-grade equivalency.

As I've moved up to a sophomore to senior class this year, Khan Academy and our blended learning approach has allowed us this year to creatively meet the needs of our students.

First, we are able to meet the needs of students that have a broad range of math skills. I can balance students from third- to twelfth-grade equivalency, in multiple subject areas, in one class.

Second, students learn at their own pace, and if they don't pass a particular subject area, they can repeat without having to start from square one. A handful of students that failed Geometry in regular education are finding success in our blended learning special education class. If a student falls behind in a typical regular education math class, they have a hard time catching up. One fifth-year senior would typically cut class once he fell behind. This year, even though his attendance is spotty, he can work at his own pace when he returns to catch up with the content. He no longer feels a need to cut class and, after two failed attempts at Geometry, will most likely pass it this semester.

What are your next steps?

Having put in place a good technology foundation, I'm now turning my attention on a few projects that are important to me.

First is the special education honors graduation statistics. At our school, we see about 40 percent of the senior class graduate with honors, cum laude or above. Typically, the honors graduation rate among special education students is 0 percent. Although we had two honor graduates last year (I believe a first), I'd like to see that number rise to four or five. I appreciate that Mr. Carganilla allowed me to implement a few creative ideas to hopefully see this idea come to fruition.

Another project we're working on is trying to create a YouTube math channel (Govs Math Lab). We were able to win grant money this year to purchase digital media equipment for our class, and my students are in the process of creating math instructional videos—project-based learning at its finest, hopefully. Mr. Carganilla also set aside additional funds to support this endeavor.[1]

Please tell us about something you've learned about blended learning and any adjustments you've made as a result.

It hasn't been easy implementing these changes. I completely changed my teaching style from being the "sage on the stage" to the "guide on the side." There are definitely some things that you want to do and avoid doing in the class if you're making changes and implementing blended learning.

Although technology affords us many advantages, one of the distinct disadvantages of technology is that it tends to isolate students. I knew I needed to be mindful to not just plop the students in front of a computer and expect them to learn. I needed to have a system that creates mindful interactions.

I have daily and weekly interactions among the students and class. On a daily basis, I often will have students work in pairs and peer-tutor each other for fifteen minutes. To have a break and interact with each other is so very important, especially with long periods and short attention spans. I would also have weekly team-building exercises where we'd discuss various topics—sometimes serious and sometimes whimsical.

To motivate my students, I constantly talk about the data and provide multiple ways for students to monitor and track their progress. I assess them using STAR Math at the beginning, middle, and end of each term, and I sit down with each of them and go over the data. When I do, we also talk about their goals and go over their term GPA, cumulative GPA, and its relation to their overall goals.

I produced study guides for Arithmetic, Pre-Algebra, Algebra, and Geometry, so that they can track their progress with Khan Academy. For me, it's just more meaningful when students track their progress with something tangible, something we can use during our weekly teacher-student meetings.

These study guides also tie in with our bulletin board that tracks the progress of all students. One of the nineteen values of Aloha is "Kulia I Ka Nu'u," which in Hawaiian means "Strive for the summit." As the students progress in Khan Academy, they mark their progress in their study guides, and they mark their progress on our bulletin board, a mountain that begins at 10 percent and moves higher and higher to 100 percent.

What advice would you give others who want to try blended learning?

In my opinion, for teachers that want to incorporate blended learning into their classrooms, they should start by reading Wes Kieschnick's book, *Bold School*. His chapter on blended learning covers all the essentials and he's very teacher-focused!

Also, it is very important that the school has systems in place to support these kind of creative classroom initiatives. If your goal is to be truly student-focused, and your school doesn't have those systems in place, you just have to do what needs to be done. You can explain or apologize later!

First, it's very important to have someone that can take you from where you are, to where you want to be, and show you a clear path to get there. As a renewal specialist, I appreciate you being patient and sticking with me for two years. Although the timing wasn't right initially, when I was ready, you showed me a different path I could take. I needed more than words in a book. I needed to see with my own eyes what blended learning looked like before I could go "all in" and you provided that.

This is the second and, in my opinion, maybe the most crucial aspect of successfully implementing blended learning: I have had 100 percent support from my principal, Mr. Carganilla. I have worked for twenty years at Farrington High School, and he is the best administrator I have ever worked with or for! I feel safe expressing my opinions and sharing my ideas at all times around him.

Some ideas are good, some are silly, but Mr. Carganilla lives his "pre-forgiven" mantra, and I feel I can be creative in such an environment and I feel I can constantly push my boundaries further. I don't know what a "Model School" blended learning classroom is supposed to look like, but I have the freedom and support in trying to create one.

Third, provide teachers with competent support in class, when needed. In all of my years at Farrington High School, I've never asked for an educational assistant. This year, I knew I needed one, especially with all of the big projects I wanted to accomplish this year. I'm so very blessed to have the most knowledgeable and competent EA I have ever met assist me: Mr. Martin.

Fourth, it's also important to have the support of everyone involved—principal, VPs, department head, registrar, schoolwide testing coordinators, fellow teachers, etc. Communication breakdowns or pushback from fellow staff members can really take the wind out of your sails. Bringing a radical new idea to fruition is like bringing a new baby into the world—you got to protect the baby. Not everyone understood what I was trying to accomplish, so in some cases I just did what needed to be done and explained it later.

Fifth, develop a comprehensive K–12 plan to meet the math needs of the students and improve communication between high school and the feeder schools. The first time I tested the arithmetic skills of my freshmen using several assessment programs, I was shocked. For example, one of my girls only knew 30 percent of her addition math facts and about 12 percent of her multiplication math facts, from 1 to 10.

How in the world, under normal conditions, was I supposed to get her Algebra ready in ninety days, with a second-grade math equivalency? If you've never been able to easily test your students' arithmetic knowledge or had a program to develop their skills, I recommend finding a program that you can use to triangulate the data.

As a side note, I hope that elementary math teachers reading this will understand the power of simple things. Math flash cards, as simple as they are, could do so much to improve the math skills of our students. Please don't let your students move on from elementary without holding them accountable to memorize their addition, subtraction, multiplication, and division math facts. They will be so much more successful in middle school and high school if they have a good foundation.

I want to close with a few sobering thoughts. I have an advisory class with sophomore Health Academy students this year. I consider these students among the best and brightest at our school. The average GPA among these students is about 3.0, meaning nearly all of these students are college and career ready. When I averaged the GPA of all of my special education students this first quarter, including from sophomores to fifth-year seniors, the average GPA was roughly 1.7, meaning, none of them are college ready. (In reality we have a few, but I'm talking on average.)

I would argue that our school or system is not unique in these respects. I'm certain that you will find similar statistics all over America.

They say that Algebra 2 is the biggest predictor of college success. I would argue that Algebra 1 is the biggest predictor of Algebra 2 success. I would also argue that math is the biggest reason why special education students don't graduate within four years from high school and don't achieve honor roll status like their regular education counterparts.

We must all take greater responsibility for our students' success, and we must adapt and change when necessary. Lack of basic skill development at the elementary levels will almost certainly lead to low achievement at the high school level. However, I have used Google Classroom, Khan Academy, STAR Math, and to a lesser extent Imagine Learning/Big Brainz to produce some amazing results among my special education high school students. It doesn't matter if you teach math, English, science, or social studies, etc., blended learning can have a positive effect on your students and you can design creative and unique approaches that are right for you and your students. If you can't find someone that is doing what you want to do, be a trailblazer and blaze a new path for others to follow.

Table 13.1.   Strategies for Building a Positive Culture

Strategy: *Blended Learning*
Sean Witwer, Special Education Math Teacher, Grades 9–11

This strategy links to the following brain-based research from the chemistry of culture characteristics in chapter 3:

  2. Release control.
  3. Create "challenge stress."
  4. Recognize excellence.
  6. Intentionally build relationships.

Blended Learning is a powerful strategy and teaching tool because it allows a teacher to leverage technology to deliver personalized instruction.

By using computers, a teacher can deliver course content through direct instruction and differentiate according to the student's individual needs. In a blended learning classroom, a teacher transitions from a "sage on the stage" to a "guide on the side" as students are empowered with greater responsibility for their own learning.

Brain research has shown that when we do make time for students to *intentionally* build relationships, both their performance and work satisfaction improve.

To successfully release control, we must learn how to create high but attainable goals, define exactly what success looks like with clear expectations . . . and then get out of the way. Being trusted to figure things out is a big motivator. When students are given more choices about which projects they'll work on and/or how they'll represent their work, their engagement and motivation increase.

Not all stress is created equal. When a teacher gives a student, or group of students, a difficult but achievable assignment, the stress of the task releases the neurochemicals oxytocin and adrenocorticotropin in the brain. These brain chemicals have been shown to help students focus and strengthens their social connections.

Step 1: Assessment (Beginning of year)	**Assessment of math skill using STAR Math.** Students' math skills are assessed at the beginning, middle, and end of each term to determine placement.
Step 2: Placement (Beginning of year)	**Math ability levels determine educational placement.** Students with lower ability levels are placed in Arithmetic. Students with higher ability levels are placed in Pre-Algebra.
Step 3: Communicate Daily Objectives	**Daily agenda is communicated to students via Google Classrooms.** Each day, daily agenda and learning objectives are communicated using Google Classrooms.
Step 4: Deliver Instruction	**Course content and instruction is delivered via computers (Releasing Control).** Students learn online using Chromebooks. Course content and instruction is delivered using Khan Academy and Big Brainz. Chromebooks are used to leverage technology for personalization.

(continued)

Table 13.1. (*continued*)

Step 5: Peer Tutoring	**Daily peer tutoring is incorporated to foster relationship building/community, collaboration, and provide assistance (Empowering Others).**

- Students work together in teams of two (occasionally three) for fifteen minutes.
- Students are paired in high-low groups, with advanced student as the "expert," helping partner.
- "Timekeeper" in class calls out when "tutoring time" begins and ends.
- Allows for mental breaks.
- Provides needed assistance. Instructional videos and "hints" may not always be enough to help struggling students.
- Develops leadership skills within a class.
- Opportunity to learn social skills. Guys that used to tease each other in middle school and would be written up for disciplinary reasons first semester are now seen as valuable assets. "Troublemakers" are often some of the smartest students and most caring if given the opportunity.

Step 6: Team Building	**Weekly "team-building" activities to help develop relationships (Build Better Relationships).**

Once a week, students are given a think-write-share activity. A random question or journal prompt is given at the beginning of class. Oftentimes it is something that has nothing to do with math. After thirty minutes of work, the class will take a break to discuss their responses. This activity is very important to first teach social skills, such as how adults interact with each other within a group. It is also important to learn that every person's ideas are important, as many of the students I work with have been marginalized at some point.

Step 7: Daily Exercise	**Daily exercise is an important component of my blended learning classroom (Build Better Relationships).**

Students are encouraged to do jumping jacks and push-ups periodically throughout the class to maintain peak mental performance.

Teacher and students regularly gather and exercise together in groups.

Note

1. Mr. Witwer's special education students have created their own YouTube channel, Govs Math Lab, to produce and share videos teaching math concepts and skills to other students:

www.youtube.com/channel/UCLNNGO28gge7rUBNXXP2XKw
www.youtube.com/watch?v=bBqwQ5Rdpd4&t=35s
www.youtube.com/watch?v=DG7jCnewZbU&t=49s
www.youtube.com/watch?v=cmHomjSmTIc&t=25s
www.youtube.com/watch?v=XT4R-HKnkaU&t=4s
www.youtube.com/watch?v=e6236xzne_E
www.youtube.com/watch?v=rAi4aHxWVKY&list=PLb7K7_bLGIpAasBRARzAWv_LeOqxhiCXx

Empowering ELLs

Norman Sales didn't choose to teach the ELL class. He thinks the class chose him. Norman started at Farrington as an educational assistant with the SPED Department in the spring of 2013. And when he earned his teaching certification in May of that year, he started applying for teaching positions.

He started interviewing for teaching jobs a couple of weeks before the 2013–2014 school year started and didn't get an interview at Farrington because there were no open positions. But he kept trying. He interviewed at schools across Oahu, James Campbell in Ewa, Leleihua in Wahiawa, and finally received an offer from Kaiser. Suddenly, right after his interview at James Campbell, Farrington called and offered him a long-term sub position covering a ninth-grade English Language Arts class. He took the offer and took his time driving to his next interview.

Norman didn't see his classroom until right before the bell rang on the first day when his first class walked into his first classroom. He also still didn't have any idea that the class was a sheltered, or J, class. In a J Class, the teacher has all ELL students and the students are learning the same English Language Arts curriculum as everyone else, but they are all grouped together, sheltered.

He also found out later that he was also working with the J Hale (House), where he shared the students with a social studies J teacher, two math J teachers, and a physical science J teacher. Although his first year was rough at times, he made it through and couldn't wait to come back the following year. Norman explains, "It all seems somewhat serendipitous now, and may sound too cheesy, but I'm really glad the class chose me."

Norman is now in his sixth year of teaching the class and does not think of switching classes anytime soon. He's connected with so many students whose stories are similar to his own. He moved to Hawaii from the Philippines in 2012 and felt like an infant in his new home. He is often still learning and acclimating at the same time as his students. He speaks the languages that the majority of his students speak. He knows and understands the culture of the households that they come from.

As an English Language Learner too, he can connect with them in a special way. Norman says, "More than anything, I want to help my students so that they can transition to the mainstream classes, maybe to the early college classes, and maybe to the AP classes. I want them to have the opportunities that may be difficult for them to achieve if they do not test out from the WIDA at the end of the year. I want them to be successful."

Interview with Norman Sales

What are some of your biggest successes?

One of my biggest successes is the higher percent of students exiting the ELL program. When I started teaching the class in 2013–2014, just 47 percent exited. In 2016 we had a 78 percent exit rate. I know these are just numbers, but I take pride in the numbers. I also know that there are numerous other factors in these passing rates, but I am proud nonetheless.

I have also seen my students in AP classes with some of them taking AP English Language and Composition and AP English Literature and Composition. The AP Language teacher this year just told me that one of her current students wrote his gratitude essay to me.

Another success is that I've engaged my students in rigorous lessons and activities. I'm proud that teachers from Farrington and other schools come and observe how I conduct my academic discussions with ELLs. My ELLs have presented at a faculty meeting about a Quad D lesson project they worked on collaboratively with students in the art classes.

A recent personal success for me was when some of my students told me I ask difficult questions! I like to say that they meant I ask rigorous questions because they said that to me after I asked them if the author we were reading at that point achieved his purpose.

Professionally, I think a success is becoming a teacher leader. I joined the Farrington Teacher Leadership Cadre, TLC, last year and have returned for a second year. I am hoping to remain in TLC as long as possible. My colleagues also voted for me to lead the ELA department this year. I am at a position where I can advocate not only for my ELLs but all our GAP students.

What have been some of the biggest barriers you have encountered teaching ELL students?

Since I attended school in the Philippines my entire life, one of the biggest challenges I had to overcome is the diversity of the classrooms here in Hawaii. I went to school with people from my small hometown and I was taught by Filipino teachers. There is also the ethnic diversity. At first, I didn't know how to reach my non-Filipino students. There is the diversity of skills even if everyone is ELL. I didn't know how to address all the evident and unnoticeable differences that were present in my classroom. Because of that diversity, my classroom management wasn't strong when I started teaching.

Also, my teacher preparation was in teaching English and not in language acquisition and development, which I think are as important as my ELA curriculum. I feel bad for the first group of kids that I taught because I didn't know many strategies that would have helped them test out. I started taking professional development seriously. My mentors, Jessica Kato, Angie Koanui, and Sherilyn Waters, were really helpful. The ELL department at Farrington is collaborative. A lot of people think I am with the ELL department, but I am actually, and was always, with the ELA department. Maybe that says a lot about the work I do with the ELL kids.

The most recent barrier is when WIDA transitioned to computer-based testing and when the State of Hawaii changed the requirements for kids to test out, making it hard to compare data over time. I am still trying to figure out how best to help my students since the testing change in 2017.

You mentioned your shock at discovering Hawaii's incredible diversity compared to your hometown in the Philippines. I know that, like most mainlanders, until I began working here in the islands, I had no real appreciation either. Can you tell us a little more about what that diversity looks like in your classroom?

I've only been teaching sheltered English classes at Farrington. Even if they are all ELLs, their abilities and experiences vary. Some of them are long-term ELLs and some of them are recent immigrants from the Philippines, Chuuk, or the many other islands in Micronesia and Polynesia. The ethnic diversity is also another thing that I wasn't used to. Back home, we all shared the same practices and traditions. The cultures of my students are also diverse. And when I say culture, I am not only referring to ethnicity or race. Their culture is complex: I have students who are gamers, some of them listen to K Pop, some of them are into visual arts, there are basketball players, and so on. There are other cultural aspects that are hidden from the surface—students view gender roles differently, discussion etiquette varies from student to student, and socio-economic backgrounds. They also have similarities. Many of my students talk about family separation through divorce, separation, or immigration. Even that contributes to the diversity in the classroom.

How has your work with Farrington's Teacher Leadership Cadre helped you to manage the diversity?

I've only been with TLC for the last two school years, but I always enjoyed collaborating with my English team and other teams that I'm involved with. Overall, work with my colleagues has broadened my skills as a teacher because the teachers I work with come with various experiences and expertise. I've been more confident in taking risks in the classroom because I know people support me. Also, we often have difficult conversations on pedagogy that challenge my practice, my beliefs, and my values. TLC is a group of bold leaders who are willing to try new things. This work has really helped me see the classroom differently from a one-size-fits-all to differentiation, to culturally responsiveness, to inquiry, and to other things. The atmosphere in my classroom has also tremendously changed since I started in 2013. I can confidently say that there are better relationships in my classroom. My students are also more engaged in relevant and rigorous work because I've become a more confident teacher. I owe this to my mentors, the collaboration with my teams, and the empowerment from TLC.

Can you tell us a little more about how you use www.socrative.com in class? And how have the students responded?

Here's how I've used Socrative:

1. I would create a "Short Answer" prompt from the teacher dashboard. It could be as simple as generate three universal questions. Students have unlimited chances to turn in responses.
2. Students generate questions on their team and they turn in individual questions through their phones or a computer.
3. Once all questions are turned in, there's a discussion on the quality of the questions. Which one would yield to more conversations and

more literal questions are addressed. Students also have the chance to consolidate similar questions.

4.* Once questions are narrowed down through answering literal questions and through narrowing down similar questions, students then vote on which questions they want to talk about in the succeeding discussion.

5. Students take the chosen questions back to their groups and they prepare by answering and looking for evidence.

What one thing would you suggest to any new ELL teacher starting out?

I am often frustrated. I've developed a habit of taking a break to take a deep breath in the middle of a class activity just to reboot. The frustration sometimes come from plans that are failing or from another million things that are happening in the classroom. Sometimes progress takes a while to be evident in student work, interactions, and observations. And that for me is frustrating.

In other words, patience is key. And I know teachers are the most patient individuals in this universe, but ELL teachers or content-area teachers who are teaching ELLs must carry an extra dose of patience every day. The student who rarely speaks may not start interacting with everyone in the classroom until April (school year in Hawaii ends in May). You may have a new student moving to your classroom from a different teacher after finding out that the student is misplaced or a new student from another country a week before the WIDA test. You'll have a student who will be copying all his or her responses from the text you are reading because the student doesn't have an idea of plagiarism, inference, or textual evidence. There will be other factors too, just like changes in the curriculum or assessments.

But do not let your patience run out. It's worth it once you see progress, and do not forget to celebrate the small victories.

Table 14.1. Strategies for Building a Positive Culture

Strategy: *ELL Academic Discussions (Harkins Discussions)*
Norman Sales, Ninth-Grade ELA/ELL

This strategy links to the following brain-based research from the chemistry of culture characteristics in chapter 3:

2. Release control.
3. Create "challenge stress."
4. Recognize excellence.

Students can't talk if the teacher never stops. Learning to release control in the classroom is a powerful strategy for the twenty-first-century classroom. Designing lessons that allow for all students to do the thinking and working through collaboration and peer learning is essential for ELL students.

But it's not enough for students to just talk. The key to this strategy is in applying a structured process that increases ELL students' use of academic language. This strategy links directly to Culture Characteristics 2, 3, and 4 we identified in chapter 3 from Paul Zak's neuroscience research.

*Norman's Academic Discussion Strategy can be even more effective when combined with variations of Thuy Huynh's Classroom Collaboration Strategy in chapter 15. Thuy also teaches over 60 percent ELL students. Her strategy provides an excellent process and protocol that will improve the ability of ELL students to work effectively in collaborative groups.

Step 1: Direct Instruction (Beginning of the year)	*Note: Direct Instruction (DI) in this context involves devoting a specific amount of time for the students to use the moves. For example, I spend a week asking students to use language that restates a peer or language that requires them to invite a peer.* DI for levels of questioning begins with students just asking literal questions, then they progress with the levels of questions that they ask. Depending on the levels of students in the classroom, I'll require certain students to ask literal, interpretive, or universal questions, but everyone in the classroom is required to answer those questions.

• **Student Discourse Moves*:** Introduce the following discourse moves: Tell and Explain, Clarify, Restate or Summarize, Compare, Support, Build on, Question or Challenge, and Invite.
* stem4els.wceruw.org/resources/Student-and-Teacher-moves.pdf

The first seven discourse moves are from stem4els, and I added the "Invite" move in response to the CCSS Comprehension and Collaboration Standard 1C, which encourages students to "actively incorporate others into the discussion."

• **Questioning:** Students learn to ask three different types of questions: literal, interpretive, and universal questions.

Scaffolding: Provide students with scripts while learning the Student Discourse Moves. They will sound rehearsed during their first discussions, but they will begin to subconsciously use the language as they progress through the year or semester. Similarly, question stems at the beginning of the year or instruction help them construct meaningful and engaging questions. |

(continued)

Table 14.1. (*continued*)

Step 2: Close Reading	• **Close Reading Strategy:** Students use Notice & Note* and AVID's Marking and Writing in Margins. *Notice & Note @ www.heinemann.com/products/e04693. aspx • Students close read a passage or a chapter using a close reading strategy and a purpose. I've found success in using Notice & Note. Their purpose for reading depends on the objective of the discussion. Students may focus on character development while close reading an excerpt from a novel or the author's reasons and evidence while reading nonfiction. **Scaffolding:** Provide bookmarks that prompt the students to question their reading. For example, when they notice that King repeatedly uses the phrase "unjust law" in Letter from Birmingham Jail, the bookmark prompts the students to respond to the question: "Why does this keep happening again and again?" There's a bookmark in Beer's and Probst's Notice & Note.

Step 3: Generating Questions	• **Generating Questions:** Students generate interpretive and universal questions after close reading.
	  ◦ They turn in their questions to Socrative*.
	  ◦ Socrative allows teachers to delete inappropriate questions and repeated questions.
	  ◦ After all students have sent their questions, read and discuss what each question is asking. This allows the teacher and the students to clarify vocabulary and ideas.
	  ◦ The class votes for three questions that will be the focus of the upcoming discussion.
	    *Socrative: https://www.socrative.com/
	Scaffolding: I allow students to generate questions in heterogeneous groups, but I also provide the option for students to work independently.
	Responding to Questions: Students respond to all three questions. Require students to use textual evidence from their reading. This is individual work, but struggling students may be grouped with advanced or proficient students.

Step 4: Discussion Groups	**Discussion Groups:** This is critical to the academic discussions. Triads and pairs are best for initial classroom discussions, but the goal is to have all students participate individually at the end of the year.

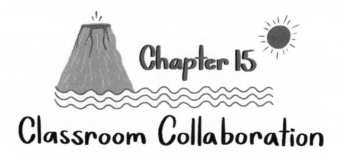

Chapter 15

Classroom Collaboration

Creating Classroom Collaboration

Full disclosure here: in this final chapter, we're going to break our pattern again. This is the only teacher and strategy in the book that does not come from Hawaii. But you'll see why we're making an exception for Thuy Huynh (Too-ee When).

First, Thuy is simply one of the most effective and inspiring teachers you will find. Thuy is a master of creating classroom collaboration for her ELL students. Also, her life story and struggle to become a teacher represents everything this book is about, and our story of A'o would not be complete without honoring her.

Thuy is a tiny woman with a calm and quiet manner. She is difficult to pick out if you were to observe her sixth-grade classroom. You see, Thuy is a master of her student-led, collaborative learning strategy, one where she quietly guides from the side, as students do the thinking, working, and talking. During every visit, her students' level of engagement and excitement about learning is contagious. It is clear from the academic language being used and rigor of the questions that students are asking their peers that this is the normal "way of work" in Thuy's classroom, and not being done for show. It's even more impressive when you learn that over 60 percent of Thuy's students are ELL, many starting at the lower levels of acquisition.

Thuy Huynh was born in Danang, Vietnam, during the Fall of Saigon, the fifth child in a family of five children. Thuy's father was taken to the Communists' prison when she was barely six months old. He was in this prison for thirteen years. Thuy's mother found herself alone as she struggled to provide her five children with the necessities of life.

Even though life was extremely difficult, Thuy vividly remembers that her mother was always supportive of her children's education. She made sure they attended school. She even found a way to provide them with special tutoring so that they could get the extra help needed to do well in school. From the start Thuy loved school. She was an outstanding student and very involved in school activities. Thuy's fellow students recognized her love of learning, and she was elected the class president every year from first grade to the ninth!

At the end of the ninth grade, Thuy's life took a dramatic turn. That year her mother somehow found a way for the family to leave Vietnam and start a new life in America. Thuy believes it was her success in school, being recognized as good student, and her involvement in school activities that gave her the confidence she needed to begin working on her English-speaking skills so she could succeed in America!

Thuy understands firsthand that starting a new life in America, with limited English, is extremely hard. She remembers how her tongue got very tired after sixth months learning the strange new language. She began to doubt whether she could achieve her childhood dream of becoming a teacher, particularly after she was told it would take at least seven years to become fluent in English. However, Thuy clearly remembers Mrs. Benton, her ESL teacher at Wilcox High School in Santa Clara, California, saying to her, "By the time you become fluent in English, you could become a teacher, because it takes that long to study." Thuy took her words to heart and decided to pursue her only dream.

Today, Thuy lives with her husband, two children, and her extended Vietnamese family in San Jose, California, and teaches at Ramblewood Elementary School in the Franklin-McKinley School District. Thuy said, "Honestly, I don't know what I would have done if I wasn't a teacher."

Interview with Thuy Huynh

Every time I've observed your classroom, one thing always stands out to me. Even though I know you have a high percentage of English Language Learners, I have a hard time identifying them. Can you please explain how you think your collaboration strategies support these ELL students in particular?

As described in my strategy, the grouping I've created is always heterogenous so students whose English is more limited can learn from others whose English is better. Besides, students need to use task cards so that everyone in the group is contributing their part to the assignment. In addition, students are strongly encouraged to use collaborative framed sentences that give them different choices in how they start their sentences. Also, before they start working in their groups, I do model how the task cards are properly used. For instance, the one that has more difficulties with English can be assigned a task that requires less language while others can do other tasks that require more language. This allows students to feel more comfortable when working in their group.[1]

As an English Language Learner yourself, what personal experiences do you think had the biggest impact on you as a teacher today?

I think the knowledge I have from my first language helped allow me to pick up my second language faster. I've always reminded myself to monitor how I speak and write by paying attention to how native speakers speak/write because I know monitoring is one of the best ways to get better at it. Even today,

I still monitor my speaking and writing. I remember when I had to turn in a writing assignment in college, I sought help by going to see a tutor in college for proofreading; when I had to do a presentation, I had to *practice, practice, and practice* my speech aloud until I felt comfortable. Thus, I can say that since monitoring and extra practice allowed me to get to my comfort zone, I've asked my students to embrace the same ideas and to apply them to their learning.

Can you tell us a little about how you approach reading to ensure all students, including ELL students, succeed?

There are two separate reading goals for my students: fictional and informational. As for fictional reading, the reading goals I set for my students are that not only do they need to learn the very basic skills in a fictional text such as literary elements or character analysis, but they also need to go beyond the basics and be able to identify, analyze, and/or compare/contrast the common parts that most stories have, such as suspense, themes, point of view, part of the story in relation to the whole, etc. Once students are able to recognize these skills on their own, they can begin to automatically apply them to any stories that they are reading. They no longer have to stop and think about them as they already have them in mind while reading, and they've rather become "automatic" to students. However, before they can begin to use these skills on their own, many model lessons need to be taught.

As for informational reading, what I want from my students is similar to that of the fictional reading. Not only do they need to learn the literal comprehension such as main idea, supporting details, summary, vocabulary, etc., but they also need to be interpretive and analytic readers such as being able to synthesize cross text, comparing/contrasting two or more books, analyzing perspective, etc. Once these skills have become automatic to students, they can apply them to whatever text they're reading.

Finally, what advice would you give any teacher who wants to improve how students collaborate effectively in pairs or groups?

I would say that teachers need to model to students how to work in pairs/ groups and to allow students opportunities to apply those skills in their own group. Also, teachers need to help students set team rules/norms and have clear tasks for each member so that all team members are focused on the assigned task. In addition, teachers need to see the conflicts from each group and to make group changes when necessary. However, to avoid conflicts, students are strongly encouraged to use collaborative-framed sentences that give them different choices in how they start their sentences.

Table 15.1. Strategies for Building a Positive Culture

Strategy: *Creating Classroom Collaboration*
Thuy Huynh, Sixth-Grade ELL

Step 1: Formal and Informal Assessment (Beginning of year)	**STAR Reading and Math Assessments and John's Reading Assessment:** Students' reading and math levels are assessed at the beginning of the school year to determine heterogenous group placement. **Teacher's Observation:** Students' behaviors, independent levels, and abilities to work with others are observed so proper grouping can be done.
Step 2: Group Placement	Students' behaviors, independent levels, and abilities to work with others determine the kind of heterogenous group that students are in. Each heterogenous group is composed of four different levels such as: • Advanced, Proficient, Basic, and Below Basic (BB) • Advanced, Proficient, Basic, and Basic • Proficient, Proficient, Basic, Basic, or BB

Step 3: What to Prepare Before Students Work in a Group of Four	*Note: Direct instructions and guided practice must take place to ensure students' understanding of the content before group work takes place. Group work is the time for peer support and for the teacher to scaffold those that need help.*
	Task Cards:
	   ◦ Laminate, color code, and hand out task cards that explain the job description of each task such as facilitator, recorder/reporter, resource manager, and task manager.
	   ◦ Ensure students' understanding of the job description.
	   ◦ Explain how to rotate roles each time they meet: rotate in counter-clockwise and students are to sit in the same seat every time they meet so a new task can be assigned to them.
	Sentence Frame Cards for Collaboration:
	   ◦ Hand out collaborative sentence frames that give students a variety of sentences to choose from; this helps them learn how to communicate with others properly.
	   ◦ Ensure students' understanding of the sentence choices.
	Rubric for Collaboration:
	   ◦ Students rate the level of cooperation and collaboration of each team member by the end of each task. Then take the group average. Teacher will keep track of each team's scores and the group with the most points earned will get the privileges of different incentives.
	Practice getting to groups:
	   ◦ To minimize lost instructional time, allow students multiple opportunities to practice getting to their group as quietly and as quickly as possible while putting on a timer for one to two minutes.
	   ◦ Group norms need to be discussed, agreed on, and recorded before actual grouping takes place.
	Model to students how to work in their group:
	   ◦ Teacher models how each of the four tasks is performed in a group of four students.
	Model to students how to do quick debrief by the end of the day:
	   ◦ Teacher allows each group to talk about what's working and what's not working in their group so that regrouping can be done.

(continued)

Table 15.1. (*continued*)

Step 4: Teacher's Role While Students Are Working in Their Group	Circulate to ensure that students are on task, know how to perform the role described on their task card, and use the collaborative sentence frames properly. Team and class points are given while circulating. Assist students with whatever work they are doing. Allow twenty to forty minutes for group work depending on the assignment. When noticing that students begin to lose focus, group work needs to stop. Make sure students are following group norms.
Step 5: Peer Checking/ Grading to Ensure Work Is Done —	Create a chart that pairs one student with another for each day of the week. Since there are five days a week, a particular student will work with five other students by the end of the week. To avoid re-creating a new chart each year, give each student a number such 1, 2, or 3. When pairing, try to create combination patterns such as 1 with 3, 1 with 32, 2 with 4, or 2 with 30 . . . so that students work with as many other students as possible.
Create a System of Peer Evaluation	Multiple charts for each combination such as Chart A, Chart B, Chart C can be made. Each chart follows its own pattern. This allows students to work with other classmates throughout the week. Team and class points are given.
Step 6: Debriefing and Celebrating	By the end of the week, students debrief again. Different incentives are given out on Fridays such as preferred activity time (students get to choose what they want to do on Friday), free homework passes, etc.

Note

1. See appendix O.

The Aloha Spirit of the Island

I want to finish where we started: by returning to the essential question of *why*—why culture matters, why you must work at it, and why we can all learn something important from Farrington High School's highly trusting, empowered, and collaborative culture.

Many sociologists, psychologists, and political scientists believe our American culture is in crisis, a complicated crisis with many layers. Our nation is more divided than at any time since the Civil War. Some of our political leaders have tried to turn one of America's greatest strengths, our multicultural diversity, into a weapon. They've demonized and demagogued anyone who is different. They've turned their back on our nation's vision of *E Pluribus Unum*: out of many, one. Using the power of social media, politicians, pundits, everyday people, all of us have helped create walled-off camps, each with an "us against them" mentality. History teaches that this path ends in a bad place—for all of us.

We learned in chapter 4 that evidence is piling up all around us that empathy is declining in our culture and the bonds of trust in our society are breaking down. Neuroscientists and psychologists are sounding an alarm about the rapid decline of empathy, particularly among the young. Some scientists say the decline of empathy and loss of related interpersonal skills is leading to a "crisis of narcissism." So I will ask you again: What happens to a culture, a society, or a country when empathy declines—or disappears? What is the relationship between the decline in empathy and the breakdown of trust in our American culture? What other changes will occur in our society when we lose the ability to not only understand but to empathize with each other? Sadly, we are just beginning to find out, and the early answers should alarm us all.

Finding answers to these questions needs to become increasingly more important to every school leader and teacher. So let me be clear: this book is absolutely intended as a call to action. The trends being documented by social scientists are too dangerous to ignore. Let me ask you another question. When the politicians, policy makers, and the general population begin to fully recognize and understand the problems created by the decline of empathy and loss of interpersonal skills in our young people, to which institution in our society do you think they will turn to fix the problem? If the past is a guide, it will be our schools.

Lest we forget, since the days of Thomas Jefferson, America's public schools have been a foundation of our democracy and our culture. America's system of free public schools is one of our greatest gifts to the world. Throughout our history, America has counted on our public schools to help each new immigrant wave become productive members of our society. Through our schools we taught each new arrival, regardless of their origin, not just to read, write, and calculate in a new language . . . we also taught them what it means to be a good, kind, and empathetic citizen. While far from perfect, we continued to improve.

What other institution could have integrated our society and advanced the cause of civil rights for all? I know because I was there. The year I started high school in Kentucky was the first year we integrated the schools. For the first time in Kentucky history, little white boys and girls went to school side by side with little black boys and girls. While far from perfect, we continued to improve.

What other institution could have promoted equal rights and pay for women? From classrooms to the athletic fields, our schools offered opportunities to women that were not available elsewhere in our society. They helped open doors that can never be closed. While far from perfect, we continued to improve. At this point in history we need our public schools once again. And to do what?

This book certainly does not have all the answers to that question, but it can offer a start. We have explored successful strategies that anyone can use to create a more positive and empathetic culture by building stronger relationships with those around us. Science is on our side. Neuroscientists tell us that we can not only slow the rate of empathy decline in our students, teachers, schools, and communities, we can reverse it.

Empathy is like a muscle we can make stronger with exercise. And we can start by learning from those who have already grown stronger. We can learn something about exercising empathy, about building a positive culture from strong relationships, and trusting in trust. We can learn from the Farrington Way and their incredible ability to celebrate and unite so many diverse cultures.

Let me be crystal clear. Farrington High School is far from perfect. It will always be a work in progress that is never done. Culture is built every day from the collective relationships in a classroom or school. We choose our culture each day in the same way that we choose our attitude. Farrington simply chose to put relationships, empathy, and culture first. While far from perfect, they continue to improve.

We can learn from the culture of Hawaii as well because Farrington is so deeply rooted in the history of the Kalihi immigrant culture. The story of the Kalihi community may be one of the best ways to understand the real Hawaii, a small speck of land in the middle of the world's largest ocean. As I've noted previously, Hawaii's story has more than its share of sadness, dishonesty, destruction, and greed. Sadly, those human failures are found everywhere, even in paradise. But to focus on them is not the Farrington Way, for Farrington follows its own mantra. At Farrington, you are pre-forgiven and the Aloha Spirit is as real as the palm trees.

At Farrington, Aloha is not a tourist slogan, nor is the word a part of the many languages spoken on campus. Ultimately, native Hawaiian students and teachers make up only a small minority. But all Farrington students are taught empathy, to celebrate and value their diversity. They are not asked to abandon the culture of their "home island." While honoring themselves, they are taught to find what is good in all cultures, including their new home: Hawaii. While far from perfect, they continue to improve.

I have traveled Hawaii for ten years. Nowhere have I found a deeper expression of Aloha. At Farrington, it is a way of life. Sometimes it is called "the Aloha Spirit" by native Hawaiians. The spirit of Aloha was an important lesson taught to the children of the ancient Hawaiians about the world of which they were a part. In a spiritual sense, Aloha means being a part of all that is, and that all that is is a part of me. It means to have respect for all that is in this world. To understand that the earth, the sea, and sky are mine to honor and care for.

Finally, from Farrington I've learned to understand and appreciate the wisdom of A'o. The Hawaiian concept of A'o says that teaching and learning are not separate. They are one thing; different sides of the same coin, different links in a great circle. The ancient Hawaiians believed that whenever we learned new knowledge, we received a responsibility to share that learning, to pass it on. Sharing and caring is how we close our circle. The more valuable the knowledge, the greater our responsibility to share.

With this book I have attempted to close my own circle. Aloha nui loa.

Appendix A

Growth Mindset Frayer Model

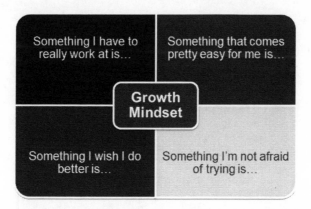

Find valuable Growth Mindset assessments at www.mindsetworks.com/assess/.

Appendix B

Empathy P-L-A-N

Prioritize It

Make empathy a leadership focus. Include empathy in your action planning. Plan for it, budget for it, schedule for it. There are many activities and exercises available online that you can use. But learning empathy, like learning any skill, needs to include practice and expert feedback over time.

Learn to Balance

In both your classrooms and school, balance digital communications and face-to-face communications. Make time to talk. Don't stop texting, but make time to talk. Consider a "no tech time" policy during some meetings that includes no mobile phones/laptop use. It is amazing the difference in attention and dialogue. Face-to-face conversations require the ability to listen and the courage to give feedback without hiding behind a text message.

Assess It Regularly

Assess the level of empathy in your classroom or school using a variety of free tools available online. Keep track over time. Survey for specifics about quality of day-to-day interactions. Self-empathy is a starting point for improving empathy. Seeking feedback on empathy should be encouraged.

Never Stop Looking for New Ways

Never stop looking for new and creative ways to become more empathetic. Farrington High School's weekly teacher-led PD sessions always start with activities designed to build better relationships and increase empathy.

Appendix C

CULTURE FRAMEWORK

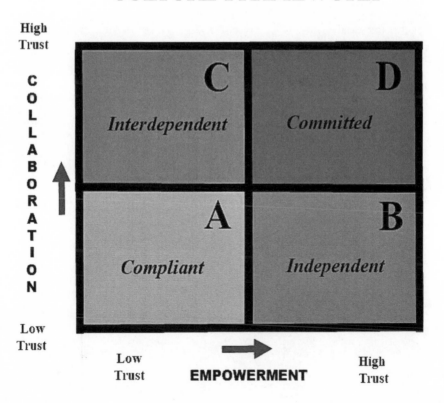

Quadrant A: Compliant

Quadrant A culture is characterized by schools with low levels of trust. When trust is at the lowest levels, both collaboration and empowerment are either not present or not very effective. Too often it describes a traditional school culture where staff works hard but a "check the box" mentality is common. Almost everyone—administrators, instructional leaders, and teachers—focus on doing only what is required; teachers acquire the skills they need and often make decisions independently.

Quadrant B: Independent

A Quad B culture is characterized by schools with higher levels of empowerment but lower levels of collaboration. In these schools, instructional leaders have managed to build greater trust with their teachers, most often by releasing control. As a result, the teachers have more freedom to experiment and try to do things their own way. While these teachers do feel trusted and empowered to try new methods, their practice is often not guided by a common set of school goals, clearly defined expectations, or even a shared vision. As a result, their instructional delivery does not benefit from being informed and improved by collaboration with others. More often, these innovative teachers work in a highly individualized and isolated environment, taking actions which may or may not be consistent with the school's vision or goals

Quadrant C: Interdependent

A Quad C culture is one where trust is high enough between teachers that they have learned to effectively collaborate. But trust is not high enough on the empowerment axis, between teachers and school leaders, that instructional leadership is broadly distributed within the school. As a result, teachers are not yet able to fully translate their collaboration into shared leadership and goal-setting around instructional practice. In a Quad C culture, too many important decisions that impact instruction often remain top-down, even as more effective collaboration offers the potential for both greater teacher buy-in to the school's goals and better problem solving to reach those goals. These schools have learned how to work smarter, not harder—but also not wiser.

Quadrant D: Committed

A Quad D culture is characterized by evidence of high levels of trust, collaboration, and empowerment by all staff, leaders, teachers, and students. These schools are unlikely to show any of Lencioni's five dysfunctions of a team. There is clear evidence that, at the highest levels of Quad D culture, both staff and students are in the habit of holding each other accountable for their own teaching and learning.

Innovation thrives in Quad D schools because their culture allows the school to change and adapt more easily through highly effective staff collaboration, which is broadly shared by a widely distributed leadership process. They are schools in which everyone shares a common vision and commitment to preparing students for the future. They are not guided solely by past experiences. In short, Quad D cultures have learned to work smarter, not harder and distribute the leadership of that work broadly.

Appendix D

The Rigor/Relevance Framework®

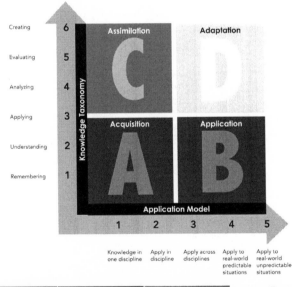

2019, International Center for Leadership in Education, a division of Houghton Mifflin Harcourt. Used with Permission.

Appendix E

The Successful Practices Network

The Successful Practices Network (SPN) is a not-for-profit organization founded in 2003 through a generous gift from Bill and Bonnie Daggett, which is committed to helping educators create a culture of rigor, relevance, and relationships for *all* students. SPN works with schools, districts, regional education centers, state departments of education, and other partner organizations to share resources (including its widely used WE Surveys that measure perceptions of students, teachers, administrators, and parent/community stakeholders about their schools), data, research (including findings from its multiyear study of best practices that was funded by the Bill & Melinda Gates Foundation), and technical assistance (including its Career and Technical Education Technical Assistance Center, which SPN operates under contract for the New York State Department of Education [NYS CTE TAC]).

To learn more about SPN, visit spnetwork.org.

Appendix F

20 Day Trust Building Action Plan

School	Principal	ICLE Coach	Date
_____	_____	_____	_____

Process:
1. Review key DSEI, Survey, and Strategic Plan data
2. Discuss successes/challenges/progress toward goals
3. Set new goals/targets, as needed
4. Create Action Plan based on needs (identify responsibilities and target date)

Analysis of Key Survey Data	
Successes	**Challenges/Focus**
1.	1.
2.	2.
3.	3.

Goals (prioritize 1-2 targets)
1.
2.
3.

Action Plan (Who is responsible, specific tasks, timeline)		
Who	Actions	Target Date

Follow-up visit (review/reflect/set goals) _____

Appendix G

Table G.1. Trust Self-Reflection Guide

I look for ways to release control to my staff.	Seldom	Sometimes	Often	Very Often
I find ways to be vulnerable with my staff.	Seldom	Sometimes	Often	Very Often
I find ways to show my staff I trust them.	Seldom	Sometimes	Often	Very Often
I practice active listening strategies.	Seldom	Sometimes	Often	Very Often
I am empathetic with my staff.	Seldom	Sometimes	Often	Very Often
I give my staff influence over things that affect them directly.	Seldom	Sometimes	Often	Very Often
I encourage my staff to take risks.	Seldom	Sometimes	Often	Very Often
I find ways to show my staff they are capable.	Seldom	Sometimes	Often	Very Often
I find ways to show my staff that I am confident in their skills.	Seldom	Sometimes	Often	Very Often
I am transparent when sharing information.	Seldom	Sometimes	Often	Very Often
I find ways to show my staff I care about their welfare.	Seldom	Sometimes	Often	Very Often

Appendix H

Farrington High School Teacher Leadership Cadre Application

Name:

Content Area:

Years of Teaching:

What qualities do you have that will allow you to provide effective professional development to the faculty at Farrington High School?

Describe a time that you exhibited the qualities of a teacher leader and/or a change agent for the school.

Tell us about an NTP session that impacted you. Describe what stuck with you and why it mattered to you.

Explain a time that you took a risk. What contributed to your decision to take that risk? How did the risk turn out?

Check the box(es) that apply to you regarding technology.

- ☐ Not comfortable using technology
- ☐ Willing to try to use technology
- ☐ Able to use most technology with support
- ☐ Able to use most technology independently
- ☐ Able to use technolgy and teach others how to use it
- ☐ Enjoy trying new technology

Is there anything else you want us to know?

Appendix I

Farrington High School Teacher Leadership Cadre Meeting Norms

Meeting Norms

1. Respectful dialogue is essential.
2. Be solution oriented.
3. Address issues, not people. Don't take things personally.
4. What happens in TLC, stays in TLC. Always present as friends.
5. Try to speak up as early as possible.
6. Be cognizant of time and don't be offended if colleagues step in to expedite conversations.
7. Listen with an open mind.
8. Support one another at all times.

Decision-Making Protocol

We will strive for consensus in all decisions. Consensus means that everyone has a chance to describe their feelings and all TLC members can live with the decision. When necessary we will determine TLC members' level of comfort with the decision using the fist to five model—a three indicates members can "live with" the decision. Facilitator will be cognizant of time and initiate checks for consensus.

Suggested Tips for Building Consensus from Adaptive Schools:

1. Insist that all views be heard, understood, and respected.
2. Legitimize all perceptions.
3. Confront problems, misunderstandings, and bad feelings in early phases.
4. Achieve agreement on the objectives before making decisions.
5. Look for little successes before tackling the problems.
6. Look for ways of breaking fixation and redefining the problem. Avoid win/lose, either/or propositions.
7. Achieve agreement on criteria before making decisions.
8. Keep summing up agreements.

Appendix J

Teacher Leadership Cadre Roles and Responsibilities

Coordinator

- Follows all agreed-upon norms
- Coordinates agenda design
- Develops group member leadership
- Supports and troubleshoots the activities of subcommittee (planning teams/presenter teams)
- Informs the group of constraints and resources
- Actively networks with various stakeholders and experts
- Participates actively as an engaged participant
- Works directly with administration
- Conferences with TLC members on a quarterly basis
- Manages all budgetary concerns
- Dares greatly and is wholehearted with others

Facilitator

- Follows all agreed-upon norms
- Remains neutral to the content
- Focuses group energy
- Keeps group on task
- Calls for consensus
- Directs processes

- Encourages everyone to participate and ensures equity of voice
- Protects participants and ideas from attack
- Contributes to agenda planning
- Elicits clarity regarding meeting followup
- Dares greatly and is wholehearted with others

Engaged Participant

- Follows all agreed-upon norms
- Monitors one's own and others' adherence to meeting norms
- Actively contributes ideas to the conversation
- Seeks and provides data
- Opens the door for others to speak
- Tests consensus
- Is conscious of one's own assumptions and knowledge and how these interfere with one's own listening
- Offers to facilitate when opportunity arises
- Is willing to be flexible for the greater good
- Follows through on commitments and asks for help if overwhelmed
- Supports others
- Dares greatly and is wholehearted with others

Appendix K

Teacher Leadership Cadre
Relationship Activities

<u>Activity</u>: *"Teaching Through The Years"*

<u>Instructions</u>: Make a long line based on years you have been teaching

Discuss: Why did you become a teacher?

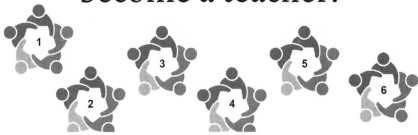

Final Product

Produce a **representation** of how your group saw the teacher in the vignette use differentiation strategies.

Possible products: skit, 3D diagram, drawing, summary on chart paper, poem

Reflection

What was the impact of working in a group with your colleagues that shared your learning style?

What impact would the differentiation strategies used today have on your students?

Share with your table what you do to differentiate the environment in your own classroom!

Evette Cruz's Community Ball (P4C)

Starting class in a circle, orients everyone's attention to the speaker.

Speaker is designated through a, "Community Ball", created by the students.

This strategy supports the norms of respect and active listening.

@GovsTLC

Charades + Pictionary

WHEN IT'S YOUR TURN:

1. Draw from red-cup
2. Choose to ACT or DRAW

THE REST OF YOUR TEAM:

- Guess which Learning Profile he/she is acting/drawing!

Strategies:
- Choice
- Flexible Grouping
- Community Building

Community Building: My content (in a brown bag)

What is your "content"? Maybe even what makes you content?

On the piece of colored paper, you will respond to **one** of the following questions:

1. Share a unique skill or quality that a lot of people may not know about you.
2. What is your life's anthem or theme song?
3. Share the story of one of your scars.
4. Share one item from your bucket list.
5. Share one of your superstitions.

Community Building: My content (in a brown bag)

1. Each group member will select another participant's "content" paper and read the question and response.

1. He/she will then guess which group member the "content" belongs to.

3. Writer of the response should identify him/herself.

Mini-Discussion 1:
Standards Based Grading

1. **Pick a question from the list to discuss for the next 7-minutes**

2. **If discussion exhausts, move on to another question**

Kinesthetic Activity: *Flip cup*

1. **Each person in your group gets a cup.**
2. **On the count of 3, everyone attempts to flip cup - Be the first to successfully flip your cup!**
3. **Repeat (2 rounds total). Keep track of who won.**

Mini-Discussion 2:
Grading Collaborative Work

1. **Pick a question from the list to discuss for the next 7-minutes**
2. **If discussion exhausts, move on to another question**

Appendix L

Teacher Leadership Cadre Working Styles Assessment

Working Styles Assessment

You will be working with UBT members and UBT staff with different working styles and backgrounds. Your working style may be very different than your co-lead's style. To work as efficiently and effectively as possible, it's helpful to assess your working style to determine the way you prefer to work.

Knowledge of Self—Working Style Self-Assessment

Teams are made up of individuals with different work experience and backgrounds, each with his or her own particular working style. There are many different working styles to think about, and every person's individual working style plays a key role in the team's development and success.

"The most important thing to remember is this: To be ready at any moment to give up what you are for what you might become."

W.E.B. DuBois

Working Style Questionnaire

Purpose

The purpose of this brief questionnaire is to get some idea of your preferred or dominant working style.

Outcome

There are no right or wrong answers and you may find that several choices appeal to you because you prefer a combination of styles.

Instructions

1. Complete the questionnaire on the next page.

2. Read each statement and order your responses with the numbers "1," "2," "3" or "4," with "1" being the response that BEST describes you and "4" being the response that LEAST describes you. Use whole numbers only (no fractions or decimals).

3. You have approximately 15 minutes to complete the questionnaire.

4. Once you have completed the questionnaire, transfer the results to the score sheet on the following page.

ACTIVITY: Working Styles Questionnaire

1. When performing a job, it is most important to me to

A [ ]   do it correctly, regardless of the time involved.
B [ ]   set deadlines and get it done.
C [ ]   work as a team, cooperatively with others.
D [ ]   demonstrate my talents and enthusiasm.

2. The most enjoyable part of working on a job is

A [ ]   the information you need to do it.
B [ ]   the results you achieve when it's done.
C [ ]   the people you meet or work with.
D [ ]   seeing how the job contributes to progress.

3. When I have several ways to get a job done, I usually

A [ ]   review the pros and cons of each way and choose.
B [ ]   choose a way that I can begin to work immediately.
C [ ]   discuss ways with others and choose the one most favored.
D [ ]   review the ways and follow my "gut" sense about what will work the best.

4. In working on a long-term job, it is most important to me to

A [ ]   understand and complete each step before going to the next step.
B [ ]   seek a fast, efficient way to complete it.
C [ ]   work on it with others in a team.
D [ ]   keep the job stimulating and exciting.

5. I am willing to take a risky action if

A [ ]   there are facts to support my action.
B [ ]   it gets the job done.
C [ ]   it will not hurt others' feelings.
D [ ]   it feels right for the situation.

ACTIVITY: Your Working Style Score Sheet

Transfer the answers from the Working Styles Questionnaire onto the scoring grid below by entering the number you chose for each letter. Next, total the columns and record the answers in the space provided.

	A [ ]	B [ ]	C [ ]	D [ ]
	A [ ]	B [ ]	C [ ]	D [ ]
	A [ ]	B [ ]	C [ ]	D [ ]
	A [ ]	B [ ]	C [ ]	D [ ]
	A [ ]	B [ ]	C [ ]	D [ ]
TOTALS:	A [ ]	B [ ]	C [ ]	D [ ]

Your LOWEST score is your preferred or dominant working style. In the case of a tied score, you should pick the working style you feel is most like you.

    A = Analytical

    B = Driver

    C = Amiable

    D = Expressive

My preferred working style is _____

TOOL: Working Style Characteristics

A–Analytical	B–Driver
Cautious actions and decisions	Takes action and acts decisively
Likes organization and structure	Likes control
Dislikes involvement with others	Dislikes inaction
Asks many questions about specific details	Prefers maximum freedom to manage self and others
Prefers objective, task-oriented work environment	Cool and independent, competitive with others
Wants to be accurate and therefore relies too much on data collection	Low tolerance for feelings, attitudes and advice of others
Seeks security and self-actualization	Works quickly and efficiently by themselves

C–Amiable	D–Expressive
Slow at taking action and making decisions	Spontaneous actions and decisions, risk taker
Likes close, personal relationships	Not limited by tradition
Dislikes interpersonal conflict	Likes involvement
Supports and "actively" listens to others	Generates new and innovative ideas
Weak at goal setting and self-direction	Tends to dream and get others caught up in the dream
Demonstrates excellent ability to gain support from others	Jumps from one activity to another
Works slowly and cohesively with others	Works quickly and excitingly with others
Seeks security and inclusion	Not good with follow-through

Your Style / Other Style	Analytical	Driver	Amiable	Expressive
Analytical	Establish priority of tasks to be done. Commit to firm time frames for your work and stick to them.	Take a deep breath, relax and slow down. With analyticals, you need to demonstrate you have considered all or most options or outcomes before moving ahead.	Cut short the social hour and get right down to the specifics. The more information you have to support your position, the better.	Translate your vision into specific tasks or goals. Involve analyticals in research and developing the details of the plan of action.
Driver	Organize your work around major themes; prepare "executive summaries" with headings or bullets that state the conclusions first and supporting data and analysis second.	Remind each other of your similarities and your need to adopt qualities of the other styles.	Don't take anything personally. Getting results is what counts with drivers; be decisive and dynamic. Emphasize the bottom line.	Take time to think about what your vision really is; translate it into action steps with objectives and timelines.
Amiable	Start off on a personal note, gravitate to project specifics and expectations; emphasize the greater good of the project.	Spend time up front gaining trust and confidence; be inclusive. Be sure to be specific about deadlines, even when it seems obvious.	Laugh with each other about how important it is being relational. Then focus on what we really need to accomplish here and do it.	Tell them how important the team concept is to making your vision a reality. Give amiables the job of team building to make the dream come true.
Expressive	Jazz up your presentation; try to think of the BIG picture. Involve the expressive in developing the "vision" or marketing of the plan.	Be patient and try to work with a flip chart to harness creative spirits. Emphasize time lines and due dates. Build in flexibility to allow the free rein of creativity.	Engage the expressive with appreciation of their vision and creativity. Harness this energy to deal with pesky but important details only they can address.	Remind each other of your tendency to generate a lot of ideas without thinking through how to implement them.

/

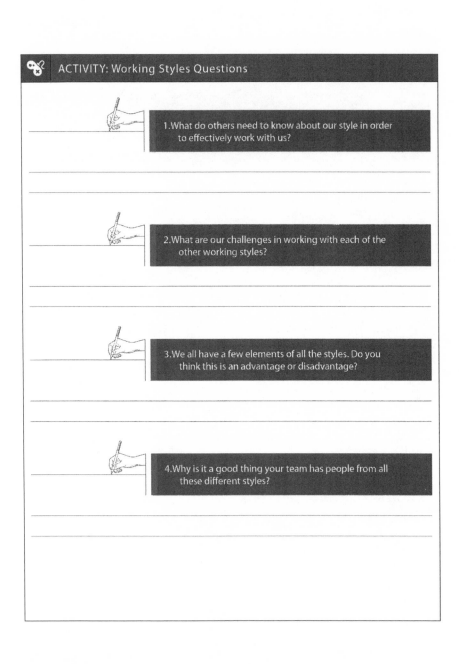

ACTIVITY: Working Styles Questions

1. What do others need to know about our style in order to effectively work with us?

2. What are our challenges in working with each of the other working styles?

3. We all have a few elements of all the styles. Do you think this is an advantage or disadvantage?

4. Why is it a good thing your team has people from all these different styles?

Appendix M

Teacher Leadership Cadre Makeup Activity

This session focused on the differentiation of content. Participants learned about the importance of physical fitness (content) through a stations activity (differentiation strategy). There were a total of four stations: a video, articles, interview, and self-reflection. You will be completing the last two sections. For the interview questions, please find another person to interview and record their responses below. Complete the self-reflection questions on your own.

Interview

What do you consider physical activities to be? Is it the same as exercise?

What could you do to stay physically active?

What kinds of activities have you or do you currently participate in that improved your health?

Self Reflection

Remember a time, when you were active how did you feel? Positive? Negative?

Did your level of physical activity change?

If you could set a goal to complete for the end of they year, regarding physical activity, what would it be? Why?

Appendix N

Teacher Leadership Cadre Makeup Activity

Directions:

1. What are your thoughts on the quote below? Do you agree or disagree with the statement and why?
   "For some students, the certainty of praise and success in school has become a drug; they continually need more. For many other students, year upon year of 'not good enough' has eroded their intellectual self-confidence and resulted in a kind of mind-numbing malaise" (L. Earl, *Assessment as Learning* [Thousand Oaks, CA: Corwin, 2003], 15).
2. Respond to any three (out of the eight) discussion questions below.

Mini-Discussion #1: Standards-Based Grading	Mini-Discussion #2: Grading Collaborative Work
1. What is your understanding of standards-based grading?	1. Does the way you grade collaborative work impact the results?
2. How does standards-based grading affect student motivation?	2. What do you do about kids who don't do as much work as others?
3. Would standards-based grading change how you teach? Why or why not?	3. How do you set up assignments to ensure a fair distribution of tasks?
4. Describe any experiences you may have had with standards-based grading.	4. What do you do to assess both the process and the product?

Appendix O

Collaboration Rubric

Directions: On a scale from 1 to 5 (1 being the lowest and 5 being the highest), please rate each team member based on the categories given below. Then return it to your teacher.

Student Name and Name of Assignment	Follows Team Norms	Is Ready to Work by Bringing Supplies and Materials	Stays on Task	Contributes and Is Helpful to Others	Respects Others by Making Good Word Choices
1.					
2.					
3.					
4.					
5.					
Average score for the entire team					

Bibliography

Alexander, Jessica Joelle, and Iben Sandahl. *The Danish Way of Parenting; What the Happiest People in the World Know About Raising Confident, Capable Kids*. New York: Penguin Random House, 2016.

Azar, Beth. "Your Brain on Culture." *Monitor on Psychology* 41, no. 10 (November 2010): 44.

Bergland, Christopher. "The Neuroscience of Savoring Positive Emotion." *Psychology Today*, July 24, 2015. www.psychologytoday.com/us/blog/the-athletes-way/201507/the-neuroscience-savoring-positive-emotions.

Box, Chris, and Mark Dawson. "Forging a Winning Culture." *PwC Financial Services* (2015): 1–16. www.pwc.com/gx/en/financial-services/publications/assets/pwc-forging-a-winning-culture.pdf.

Businessolver. "State of Workplace Empathy." Last modified January 2018. www.businessolver.com/resources/state-of-workplace-empathy#gref.

Covey, Stephen R. *The Seven Habits of Highly Effective People: Restoring the Character Ethic*. New York: Simon and Schuster, 1989.

Dolby, Nadine. "The Decline of Empathy and the Future of Liberal Education." *Liberal Education* 99, no. 2 (Spring 2013). www.aacu.org/publications-research/periodicals/decline-empathy-and-future-liberal-education.

Freeman, Jonathan B., Nicholas O. Rule, Reginald B. Adams Jr., and Nalini Ambady. "Culture Shapes a Mesolimbic Response to Signals of Dominance and Subordination that Associates with Behavior." *Neuroimage* 47, no. 1 (August 1, 2009): 353–59.

Goh, Joshua O. S., Eric D. Leshikar, Bradley P. Sutton, Jiat Chow Tan, Sam K. Y. Sim, Andrew C. Hebrank, and Denise C. Park. "Culture Differences in Neural Processing of Faces and Houses in the Ventral Visual Cortex." *Social Cognitive and Affective Neuroscience* 5, nos. 2–3 (June/September 2010): 227–35.

Guiso, Luigi, Paola Sapienza, and Luigi Zingales. "The Value of Corporate Culture." *Chicago Booth Research Paper*, No. 13-80 (September 2013): 1-45. economics.mit. edu/files/9721.

Helliwell, John, Richard Layard, and Jeffrey Sachs, eds. *World Happiness Report 2017*. New York: Sustainable Development Solutions Network, 2017. worldhappiness. report/ed/2017/.

Jones, Richard, and Kathleen Weigel. "Overwhelm Cultural Inertia: Reshape School Culture to Truly Reflect College AND Career Readiness." CTE Technical Assistance Center of NY: A Division of the Successful Practices Network (2016): 1-9. nyctecen ter.org/images/files/Publications/Overwhelm-Cultural-Inertia.pdf.

Kieschnick, Wes. *Bold School*. Rexford, NY: ICLE, 2017.

Konrath, Sara H., Edward H. O'Brien, and Courtney Hsing. "Changes in Dispositional Empathy in American College Students Over Time: A Meta-Analysis." *Personality and Social Psychology Review* 15, no. 2 (August 2010): 180-98.

Krings, Mike. "Study Shows Decline in Cognitive Empathy Among Middle School Students." *KU News Service*, October 3, 2016. news.ku.edu/mk%20empathy.

Lencioni, Patrick. *The Five Dysfunctions of a Team: A Leadership Fable*. San Francisco: Jossey-Bass, 2002.

Mattone, John, and Nick Vaidya. *Cultural Transformations: Lessons of Leadership and Corporate Reinvention*. Hoboken, NJ: Wiley, 2016.

Szalavitz, Maria. "Shocker: Empathy Dropped 40% in College Students Since 2000." *Psychology Today*, May 28, 2010. www.psychologytoday.com/us/blog/born -love/201005/shocker-empathy-dropped-40-in-college-students-2000.

Twenge, Jean M., and W. Keith Campbell. *The Narcissism Epidemic: Living in the Age of Entitlement*. New York: Free Press, 2009.

Valdes, Kristin Stuart. *Humanizing the Classroom: Using Role-Plays to Teach Social and Emotional Skills in Middle School and High School*. Lanham, MD: Rowman & Little-field, 2019.

Zak, Paul J. "The Neuroscience of Trust." *Harvard Business Review*, January–February 2017.

About the Author

Jim Warford remains first and foremost a teacher, spending more than one hundred days a year in classrooms across the country. In 1971, he taught his first class in a Kentucky Head Start Program. He taught at Vanguard High School in Ocala, Florida, for seventeen years and was named Teacher of the Year there three separate times. Since 2005, he has served as senior advisor to the International Center for Leadership in Education. In 2008, he created an online teacher training program for the University of Hawaii, Maui College.

As superintendent of Florida's Marion County Public Schools, he first implemented the Continuous Improvement Model district-wide in 2000. Within three years, school grades went from three F, eight D, and only one A school to twenty A, sixteen B, and no F schools under Florida's A–F school grading system, and the high school dropout rate was cut almost in half.

In 2003, Mr. Warford was appointed as Florida's first chancellor of K–12 public schools. As chancellor he led the creation and statewide implementation of Florida's Continuous Improvement Model, FCIM, which resulted in Florida's dramatic gains in student achievement and more than 80 percent of targeted schools moving off the low-performing list. FCIM remains Florida's required intervention for all low-performing schools.

From 2005 to 2010, he was executive director of the Florida Association of School Administrators. Mr. Warford is a dynamic educational leader and a passionate speaker who remains driven by his powerful personal story and passion for teaching and learning.